Older Is Better

"Don't Act Your Age"
Bob Hope

Photo courtesy of AT&T

Prime Time I

Older Is Better

Common-Sense Steps to a Long Life, Health, and Happiness...

Elizabeth Vierck

ACROPOLIS BOOKS LTD.
WASHINGTON, D.C.

ACROPOLIS BOOKS, LTD.
Colortone Building, 2400 17th Street, N.W.
Washington, D.C. 20009

Printed in the United States of America by
COLORTONE PRESS
Creative Graphics, Inc.
Washington, D.C. 20009

Book design by Kathleen K. Cunningham

Library of Congress Cataloging-in-Publication Data

Vierck, Elizabeth, 1945-
Prime-time: the take-control guide to your positive years — by Elizabeth Vierck.
p. cm
Includes index.
ISBN 0-87491-849-9 (pbk.) / $9.95
1. Aging. 2. Aged—Health and hygiene. 3. Aged—Social conditions. I. Title.
QP86.V53 1988 87-26458
646.7'9—dc19 CIP

Each volume of *Prime Time* salutes the media, an advertiser, or a corporation that promotes a positive image of aging. The first volume salutes AT&T.

For my mother, Elizabeth Amadon Vierck

Contents

PART TWO:

Steps to Obtain a Long Life, Health, and Happiness

Acknowledgments

While the writing of *Prime Time* is mine, the content is the reflection of the wisdom of many. The expertise and experience of the people and organizations listed below provided the genesis of this book.

I would like to thank the following people who took time out of their demanding schedules to either give me a personal interview or write me their thoughts about their lives past age 60: Bob Hope, Julia Child, Millicent Fenwick, Daddy Bruce Randolph, Louise Crooks, Maggie Kuhn, Claude Pepper, and Art Buchwald.

I have been fortunate in my years in gerontology to work with and/or interview many of the best in the field of aging. I would particularly like to thank the staff of the National Institute on Aging and its present and former directors, Franklin T. Williams and Robert M. Butler, for providing me with a wealth of material, which I have used liberally throughout the book. I am grateful to my colleagues and friends with whom I served on the staff of the US Senate Special Committee on Aging from 1981 to 1986. They contributed mightily to the content of this book and enthusiastically cheered me on through numerous drafts. The staffs of other organizations were also extremely helpful including: Aging Network Services, Alzheimer's Disease and Related Disorders Association, American Association of Retired Persons, American Association of Homes for the Aging, American Cancer Society, American Council of the Blind, American Dental Association, American Diabetes Association, American Federation of Home Health Agencies, American Foundation for the Blind, American Health Care Association, American Heart Association, American Medical Association, American Nurses Association, American Podiatric Medical Association, American Psychiatric Association, American Public Health Association, American Psychological Association, American Red Cross, Arthritis Foundation, Better Hearing Institute, Chamber of Commerce, Grey Panthers, Health Insurance Association of America, Legal Council for the Elderly, National Association of Area Agencies on Aging, National Association of State Units on Aging, National Association for Homecare, National Association of Nutrition and Aging Services Programs, National Council on Aging, National Council of Senior Citizens, National Homecaring Council, National Hospice Association, National Mental Health Association, Parkinson's Disease Foundation, and Social Security Administration.

Cynthia Vartan believed in the project long ago, but unfortunately did not get to be part of its fruition. I am grateful for her initial interest and guidance.

Last, but not least, living with a spouse who is writing a book is akin to living in a box of myopic fleas. I would like to thank my husband, Craig Boyle, for his patience, encouragement, and wisdom, without which this book might still be but a good idea.

A Note From the Author

While doing the research for and writing *Prime Time* I have been fortunate to interview or correspond with a number of older persons who have aged in a way that most of us would view as successful. They are active, vital members of their communities (for some that community is quite large; Bob Hope's community is a world stage, Louise Crooks' is the 28 million member American Association of Retired Persons). They are living long and healthy lives. They are happy.

Without exception, their secrets are all variations on what Claude Pepper refers to it as *the philosophy of animation.* The *philosophy of animation* is a philosophy of engagement with life that is so strong it wins out over any adversity that may come along. It is a philosophy of humour, vivacity and enthusiasm.

Art Buchwald, who is clearly irritated by the process of growing older, describes the *Philosophy of animation* when he says: "The only thing that makes age important is whether they require you to resign or not."Bob Hope calls it *not acting your age.* Maggie Kuhn refers to: *"a good and passionate purpose."* Julia Child says: *keeping in circulation* is the key. Louise Crooks refers to *making a better life for people less fortunate.* Millicent Fenwick advises: *"develop and don't stay frozen.* Daddy Bruce Randolph puts it in religious terms: *"give rather than receive."*

Prime Time and Acropolis Books, Ltd., would like to thank these older Americans for sharing their philosophies of animation with us.

Introduction to the *Prime Time* Series

Prime Time is a series for and about you as you age. It is also for and about your parents, spouse, family, and friends. With this century's dramatic increase in life expectancy, you and your loved ones can expect to be living with yourselves for a long time. In this country our youths are spent preparing for the changes that will take place in our adulthood — careers, marriage, and parenthood. We do not spend time preparing for the changes that will take place in older age. This series is for you if you are or plan to be growing older. It is designed to be referred to again and again throughout your older years as the need arises.

Henri-Frederic Amiel said: "To know how to grow old is the masterwork of wisdom." Throughout these pages you will find information that, with some thoughtfulness and planning, can help you prepare for and experience, not only your own aging, but that of your loved ones, with wisdom.

You will find good news and bad news here. You will find that aging does not have to be the affliction it far too often is made out to be, but that it does bring change—change that has its natural place in the life cycle along with a baby's first steps.

You will discover that change can bring advantages (good news), as well as disadvantages (bad news). But, you will find that if you or someone you love gets hit with the bad news much can be done to ease adjustment. This last point is the focus of this series. For all of us the quality of life during our later years will depend on our ability to adjust to the changes that will take place and to avail ourselves of the best information available to help make adjustments.

In the same light, many of the changes that take place in older age involve wading through a significant amount of the bureaucratic mumbo jumbo involved in Medicare, supplemental health insurance, Social Security, pension plans, and so on. You will find important information in these volumes that will help clear up much of this mumbo jumbo.

Amiel not only said that growing older is the masterwork of wisdom, he also said that growing older is "one of the most difficult chapters in the great art of living." The information in this book is compiled from the experience and knowledge that older people, scientists, and professionals have shared with me. Reflected in these pages is their wisdom, much of which may be summed by heeding Julia Child's advice, ". . . If you wait long enough old age is going to happen to you. You'd better plan for it."

Elizabeth Vierck
Denver, Colorado
December 1987

How to Use *Prime Time*

Prime Time is a five-volume series in which each volume stands alone. It is designed to be used either as a whole or each volume may be used individually for specific topics. The volumes cover the following five general topics: general information about aging (Volume I); health, safety and well-being (Volume II); finances, employment, and volunteering (Volume III); housing, independent living, and legal issues (Volume IV); and health care and health insurance (Volume V). Each volume includes extensive resources that are specific to the issues included in that volume.

Volume One, *Older is Better,* is the shortest of the five volumes. It includes general information about aging that provides the background for the consumer-based materials in the following four volumes. It also provides information on places to go for help that are key to making the other four volumes work.

The purpose of this series is to help you understand aging and the resources available to you so that you can make your older years positive ones. As you read this series you will find that

- There is much good news about aging.
- Much of what you assumed to be true about aging is probably based on myth.
- There are many things you can do to lengthen your life span and improve your health.
- If things do go wrong in your 50s, 60s, 70s, or 80s and beyond, there are many things that can be done to maximize health and increase the quality of your life.

Note to the reader: Bibliographic information has not been included in this volume. If you would like to know the reference for a particular fact referred to in the text, please write to the author in care of the publisher.

Part One

Secrets of a Long Life, Health, and Happiness

Bob Hope Doesn't Act His Age

Would anyone dispute the fact that Bob Hope is a founding father of radio, TV, and the big screen? Or that he is the patron saint of the GIs of three wars? Bob's comic, affectionate dominance of the American heart has rightfully won him numerous awards, among them four special Academy Awards.

At age 84, Hope is Hollywood's most famous golfer. He is a self-confessed addict of the little white substances known as golf balls. In his book, *Confessions of a Hooker,* published when he was 83, he says: "The beauty of golf is that you can play it long after you have given up other sports." He adds: "I still get upset over a bad shot, though, just like anyone else. But it's silly to let the game get to you. When I miss a shot I think what a beautiful day it is. Then I take a deep breath. I have to. That's what gives me the strength to break the club."

Aging has not made a duffer out of Bob Hope. He darts from airplane terminals to footlights to golf courses. He plays clubs, hotels, and universities. He produces and stars in TV specials and makes frequent star appearances. He plays in a dozen or so pro-am tournaments a year. Once a year he sponsors the Bob Hope Chrysler Classic held in Palm Springs, California.

Reflecting on aging in America, Hope says: "For years everybody thought you had to retire at 60. Then people who retired went back to work because they couldn't stand the loneliness of sitting around. And they found out that they were staying younger longer."

Bob Hope's "secret" formula? He says: "Everybody asks me how come I can still work and dance at my age and I say it's very simple . . . don't act your age.

"I've also found that a great thing is to have a few friends that you can get together with and have a few laughs. That, and a positive attitude about life are my secrets. Try to build a couple of laugh lines. They are the best kinds of lines to have."

And, we might add, how better to build those laugh lines than to listen to Bob Hope?

Julia Child's Recipe for a Healthy and Long Life

If grades were given out for planning ahead to make older years positive ones, Julia Child, 75, and her husband, Paul, 85, would get an A+. But, first some background.

Julia's career as America's favorite serious cook (she does not like the word gourmet) began when her husband became cultural attaché for the US State Department in France in the late 1940s. While in France Julia enrolled in the Cordon Bleu and then struck out on her own. With two friends she opened a cooking school for Americans and wrote a cookbook. Eventually the Childs returned to the United States and the rest is history. American cuisine and public television would never be the same again.

Julia is single-handedly responsible for raising the American standard of eating. Her first volume, *Mastering the Art of French Cooking,* written with Simone Beck and Louisette Bertholle, was published in 1961. It is still considered the English language bible of classic French cuisine. The first segment of her "French Chef" public television series aired on WGBH in Boston on February 11, 1963. Since then, she has won numerous awards for her television series, five books, and numerous articles.

Since their marriage in 1946, the Childs have been inseparable; "always together," Julia says. First, Julia was Paul's partner when he worked for the State Department, then Paul became Julia's photographer and partner for her projects. When they moved back to the US they both made mid-life career changes —from diplomats to painter photographer and serious cook/author/TV star. Together, they are now planning ahead in case they develop problems during their older years. The Childs have applied to two continuing care communities so that if one or the other "slips off the raft," as Julia puts it, they will be taken care of and no family member will need to step in. They have also made arrangements with an attorney to let them know that "the time has come" in case they happen to "slip off the raft" but still think they are afloat.

In the meantime, while feeling some age-related changes, the Childs lead active, productive, pleasant, sensible lives. Julia's knees are giving out. She has had one replaced entirely and the other will have to be replaced in another year or two. She is also beginning to get a cataract in one eye. "But, luckily, all those things can now be fixed," she says optimistically. Paul has slowed down a bit and no longer does the photography for Julia's projects. "But he's hanging in there," Julia says.

Julia is working full-time on an immense undertaking, an all new comprehensive cookbook for "the serious home cook." When that project is finished she will start a new television series and accompanying book. When asked what the Childs do for leisure, Julia replies: "We enjoy what we do and leisure is our friends and our walks and occasional trips. We very much enjoy our work so we don't need any respite."

The Childs follow advice that their doctor in Boston gave them: moderation, eating a variety of foods, weight watching, and exercise. For example, for the sake of health, Julia Child, the Master French chef, *cooks with olive oil,* not butter. They always eat "fresh food: fresh fruit and vegetables." Julia also limits alcohol to half a glass of wine for lunch and one drink and another glass of wine for dinner. Paul never drinks strong drinks. They get daily exercise. They do sitting-up exercises and walk about 25 minutes to get the paper every morning and then walk again for a half-hour in the afternoon.

Julia feels strongly about the plans she and her husband have made for their advanced years. She says: "I really have no patience with the people who have not planned for the final days. We've known several people whose parents or somebody have gone batty and they've refused to do anything. They spend the whole family fortune taking care of this ridiculous person who didn't have the wit to do something. I don't want anyone to have to bother about us. If anything happens to us I don't want to be a burden to people."

Julia offers some sound tips based on her own experience: "My advice is if you wait long enough old age is going to happen to you. You'd better plan for it. But lead as active and productive a life as you can all the time. You're lucky if what you like falls upon you, otherwise you will just have to find it. Never retire. Find something that you can do. There are all kinds of volunteer things that you can participate in. If you sit around doing nothing your mind will go foul. I've noticed myself, if you're too busy and you've got all sorts of schedules, you don't get sick.

"You can do volunteer and political work, learn the computer, learn the kinds of skills that can be useful to people. Cooking is certainly a marvelous skill. People love to be invited over. There is no excuse for being alone. If nobody asks you, you can ask them. Keep in circulation and keep knowing young people. If you don't you'll soon find everyone's dead and you'll have no friends at all. Take it seriously. Don't just say the Lord will provide. The Lord takes care of those who take care of themselves. If you don't do anything you can't blame anyone but yourself. In other words, you are the master of your fate."

Julia and Paul Child have planned ahead. They have established a healthy routine which is serving them well in their 70s and 80s. Summing up her philosophy of life, Julia offers this recipe for a healthy long life: "Moderation in all things, eating a great variety of foods, weight watching and exercise, and loving work."

Millicent Fenwick Chooses "I Don't Want To" over "I Can't"

One of the best-loved characters in Garry Trudeau's comic strip "Doonesbury" is Lacey Davenport, a pipe-smoking, feisty, patrician congresswoman. ("Oh, you poor dears," Lacey once told a group of striking blue-collar workers.) As most of Lacey's fans know, she is modeled after Millicent Fenwick, 77, grandmother and former New Jersey congresswoman. Fenwick likes Lacey. She says: "Some of the things that Lacey said were so silly, so comic, and so like me. I don't mind it a bit. Lacey is not impressed by herself or anyone else."

Lacey and Millicent may not be impressed, but most of the rest of us are. Fenwick's life is a study in glamour, wealth, tragedy, poverty, and politics. She was born into a wealthy New Jersey family and inherited a mansion that she subsequently tore down. Today she lives in its remodeled library, which has been divided into three rooms. Her characteristic pearls, tweeds, and manner of speaking exemplify her millions in "old money." But there were rough times. Her mother drowned on the *Lusitania.* During one difficult period, after a short marriage to a dandy, she was broke. And when Fenwick had two children to support, Bonwit Teller turned her down for a job because she lacked a high school diploma. (She had dropped out of Foxcroft School to accompany her father when he was appointed ambassador to Spain.) Finally she landed a job modeling for *Harper's Bazaar* and went on to be an editor for *Vogue,* where she wrote the *Vogue Book of Etiquette.* Later she became a member of the New Jersey General Assembly, served four terms in Congress (the 94th through the 97th), and recently retired as ambassador to the United Nations for food and agriculture.

Until an arterial problem grounded her in the spring of 1987, Fenwick's UN position took her to Rome, where she carried out an active schedule. She is now at home in Bernardsville, New Jersey. She recently had bypass surgery, gets short of breath and dizzy, and is unable to walk long distances. However, she finds there is a lot to do. She says she is: "drawn to the garden. I can't resist it." (Due to her condition she is not allowed to crouch and has to work sitting down.) She also serves as the honorary grandmother of her district, answers her own phone, does her own marketing, trouble-shoots for constituents who need her help, and serves on numerous committees and boards.

When asked whether she has any advise on aging, Fenwick has two messages for younger people, based on her experience with marriage and career. She says: "As a young person you are very wise if you decide on your principles, in other words, what you think is good and what is right, because if you don't you won't choose the right person to marry. And if you look at life—a good marriage is the best happiness on earth. There's no doubt in my mind. The second thing is to find an occupation that draws you. Every now and then the work ought to be so fascinating you forget lunch."

Through her personal experience, Fenwick understands and is sympathetic to the limitations that can come with age. She says: "It is very discouraging if you have something you enjoy and find that you are no longer able to do it. The key is to cherish a sense of humor."

She has some tips for her peers: "Anybody over 80 would be wise to say 'I don't want to' instead of 'I can't,' because every time you say 'I can't' you are diminished. When you are over 80 you have a right to whims. You have the freedom to say 'I don't want to.' Every time you say 'I can't' you limit yourself. I see older people who say they can't do things when their doctors say they can. They should say they don't want to. The point in life is to develop and not to stay frozen at any age."

Photo by Mary Mackey

Daddy Bruce Randolph Champions the Homeless

Eighty-eight-year-old Denver, Colorado, restaurateur and champion of the homeless, Daddy Bruce Randolph, has been featured on the "Phil Donahue Show," has had numerous articles written about him, and is the recipient of myriad awards and citations. Daddy Bruce expresses surprise and joy over his fame. Referring to the Denver street named for him, he said: "It's nice to be famous before I'm dead. Most people are dead by the time they have a street named for them."

Randolph's trademark brown bowl-like hat, his secret barbecue sauce made from a recipe drawn from the Arkansas Hills, and his generosity are local institutions. Randolph is a religious man, believing that: "the church is the heart." He lives by the biblical passage: "It is more blessed to give than to receive." He carries out his beliefs by feeding people who are hungry. Every Thanksgiving, Christmas, and Easter Daddy Bruce's Restaurant and Catering Service gives free meals to over 50,000 poor people. Over 3,000 people show up to volunteer. A local taxi company, Yellow Cab, delivers to those people unable to come to the restaurant.

The story of Daddy Bruce's life is a classic in turning adversity to advantage. The sixth of seven children of a poor family, he was born in Pastoria, Arkansas, in 1900. A childhood memory that still brings tears to his eyes is the Christmas when "Santa didn't come" because the family was too poor to buy presents. Randolph left home at 15 and eventually opened two restaurants in Pamap, Texas. He was the first black person in the town to have a restaurant in a white neighborhood. He also had a taxicab business and a hotel. When he lost his businesses in a divorce, he came to Denver and supported himself by shining shoes. He then worked as a janitor and, when his employer hired a maintenance service and fired him at the age of 62, he borrowed $1,000 and opened a barbeque catering service. After two years he opened his restaurant on a street that is now called *Bruce Randolph Avenue.* The rest is history.

Daddy Bruce's secret is that if he wants to do something he does it—it never dawns on him that he can't. This is as true as he nears 90 as it was when he was younger.

He has no plans to retire, but the Daddy Bruce Randolph Foundation has been set up to carry on his work in case anything happens to him. He is now working on plans to open a delicatessen. In the meantime he can be found at work in his restaurant, where he characteristically responds to those who thank him for his generosity: "Just say God loves you and so does Daddy Bruce."

Louise Crooks' Retirement Is Not a Time to Do Nothing

Louise Crooks, 75, the incoming president of the American Association of Retired Persons (AARP), is a resident of West Lafayette, Indiana, where she taught school for many years. Crooks' husband died from an aneurysm in 1982 just ten days before he was going to retire from Purdue University. "It was quite a shock," says Crooks.

Crooks responded to her loss by becoming an active member of AARP. She is now a major force in the nation's largest organization for older people: "I think that retirement is not a time when you should do nothing. There are lots of things that you can do. The more active you are the better you are physically and mentally," says Crooks. She elaborates: "People who retire and have no active interest in their community or world affairs or anything become rather morbid. They are not the type of people you really want to be around because everything is wrong. It's very easy to sit at home and pick everything apart and say this is wrong and that is wrong, but if you are busy you see things from a different side."

When she was younger, Crooks saw people who retired and lost interest in everything and became depressed. She says that she consciously decided: "not to be like that. I decided to find something that I would like." AARP was a perfect choice. Crooks has always been interested in people. "I was always interested in my students—that they would do well and do the best they could. I was concerned about my students and I was concerned about my country as a whole, the people in it. I feel that if I can do something to make a better life for the people who are not as fortunate as I am, then I should get out and do something. And this is what AARP is all about. I lobby, I go to Congress and testify. I don't always come out on top. We can't make all the changes we want, but we should at least try."

Crooks walks a couple of miles a day and keeps a busy schedule, traveling frequently to Washington, D.C., across the country, and abroad. She laughs at the comments she gets from her peers: "Well, you know, *people our age* should not be traveling as much. They try to tell me that I am doing too much. I can tell when too much is too much."

Crooks' term as president of AARP begins in May 1988 and will run for two years. She likes to stress the fact that AARP is not just for retired persons. Anyone 50 years of age or older can join. And AARP is working for a better life for children and grandchildren. The priorities that Crooks sees ahead for AARP are:

1. The health issue, particularly nursing home and home health care—Crooks has many letters, from women and men, who end up in poverty from trying to pay their spouse's nursing home bills.
2. The women's initiative—particularly, jobs and insurance for women who divorce in their 40s and 50s.
3. Worker equity—to teach people how to get back into the work force.
4. Minority issues—most older poor people are black, many fall through the cracks and are not eligible for needed benefits such as Medicaid.

Crooks talks passionately about the fact that people do not know that Medicare does *not* pay for many needed services such as nursing home and home health care: "We conducted a street poll and asked who would pay for care for the elderly and it was amazing how many people answered 'Medicare.' It is important to educate the younger generation so that they will prepare during their lifetime. The studies that we have done show that most younger people want better care for their parents and themselves."

When asked to give the younger generation two or three tips on how to prepare for older age, Crooks says: "If you are married, marriage is a partnership. You should know what you have—your investments, your retirement income, so that if something happens you would know what you have financially. Couples should sit down and talk this over together. And even the youngest should have a will. A second thing to do is to take care of your health. I am very happy with the baby boomers because they are taking care of their health. Take care of your health and you will have a better quality of retirement."

Maggie Kuhn Is a National Treasure

Maggie Kuhn, 83, is the force behind a national organization with international impact—the Grey Panthers. The organization is built on her philosophy of old and young working together, linking the historical perspective of the old with the energy and new ideas of the young. Through the Grey Panthers, "Maggie," as she is lovingly referred to by her admirers, has established a positive, highly visible image of aging. She is a national treasure and an internationally known example of what is possible in older age. She has almost single-handedly dispelled the myth that old age is a downhill slide.

Maggie is a small, fragile-looking woman with the Force of Mr. T. Her favorite word is "outrage." Maggie worked for more than 43 years fighting for social justice and peace in positions with the YWCA and various church groups. After so many years fighting injustice, she became a victim of injustice. At age 65, while working in the central office of the Presbyterian church to help improve race relations, Maggie became a victim of age discrimination. She was forced to retire. The church threw a party and gave her a sewing machine, implying that sewing would be a good hobby for her retirement years. Maggie responded by starting the Grey Panthers with five outraged friends. They sought to bring together the young and old to influence public policy. (The sewing machine has never been unpacked.) The Grey Panthers now have more than a hundred local networks and 60,000 members.

The Grey Panthers have worked to help improve the quality of nursing home care and to increase the availability of home care. They work to improve Social Security and Medicare and to improve the status of older women. They have worked to abolish mandatory retirement, and are now very involved in problems facing the Third World.

The Grey Panthers National Convener, as she is officially called, lives in a multi-generational household with three roommates and two cats, Charlotte and Emily. She does stretching exercises and walks every day for exercise despite "bad arthritis in her hands and legs." She needs special glasses to read due to deteriorating retinas. She is a prolific writer. She is a former editor of *Social Progress* and has written many magazine articles. She has written three books, *You Can't Be Human Alone, Let's Go Out There and Do Something About Injustice,* and *Maggie Kuhn on Aging.* The subject of two documentary films,

Maggie is currently working on her memoirs and a book on intergenerational issues.

When asked to describe her views on aging, Maggie answers with a one-liner: "Learning and sex stop only when *rigor mortis* sets in." She also says, with passion: "An indispensable aspect of productive aging is to have a good and passionate purpose. People who have turned inward do not have a goal and, in a sense, deny themselves the possibility of building on their experience. Using her work with the Grey Panthers as an example she says: "Our goal is a legacy. We're leaving a legacy of a just and peaceful society and that's of eternal value. It transcends self. We're social beings and we can't be human alone. We achieve our full humaness and realize our goals in community with others. The sad thing that I have seen in so many of my peers is their loneliness and isolation. They have not learned to reach out. Their primary community—spouse and children—die and move away and they never regroup." Asked why this happens, she says: "We lead very private lives. We don't learn about public issues. We don't get outraged enough." On the other hand, Kuhn proudly says that many women, after the loss of a spouse have learned to do just that: "There are a number of widows in the Grey Panthers whose lives have been reconstituted. Building new purposes is not disloyalty, it's the possibility of living another kind of life."

Clearly their lives and the lives of many others have been made better because of Maggie Kuhn's outrage, dedication and energy.

Claude Pepper Is a Spokesman for the Elderly

Claude Pepper, 88, spokesperson for the elderly, is a nuisance. His constant appeals to address the problems of the elderly get on the nerves of many a power-broker. As former chairman of the House Special Committee on Aging and, today, as chairman of its subcommittee on health, Pepper has been able to draw a lot of attention to the problems of the elderly and to get an impressive number of these problems solved.

Pepper is an historical figure. He was born in the first year of the 20th century, elected to an unexpired Senate term in 1936, and reelected as a Roosevelt New Dealer in 1938. As senator he promoted a program of universal health insurance and advocated civil rights, which resulted in the label "Red" Pepper. His positions led to his defeat by George Smathers in 1950 in one of the dirtiest campaigns in the country's history. Among other tricks, Smathers' supporters would plant black men in Pepper's campaign audiences and get them to go up and shake the candidate's hand while camera bulbs went off. The pictures would run throughout the state, which included large numbers of strongly prejudiced constituents. The American Medical Association (AMA) even contributed to his loss—they saw that a way to defeat universal health insurance, which they opposed, was to defeat its promoters and they poured money into the Smathers campaign. Ironically, a version of universal health insurance eventually became law as Medicare, a program that now has the strong support of the AMA. After his defeat, Pepper went back to practicing law in Miami and then won election to the House of Representatives in 1962. Out of respect, most of his colleagues, friends, and admirers still call him "Senator."

Pepper's romance with and marriage to his wife, Mildred, is a capital love story. She was described in print as: "one of the most beautiful women in Washington." In his book, *Pepper: Eyewitness to a Century,* he writes: "She was at my side when ever I needed her, which was often." Mildred died in 1979. Pepper laments: "There is a void in my life since she left, a void that can never be filled."

Pepper's achievements on behalf of the elderly are many. In 1937 he introduced a bill in the Senate called the Townsend Plan, the forerunner of Social Security. He was active and instrumental in the passage of Medicare and Medicaid in 1965. He worked in both the House and the Senate to provide federal funds for housing for the elderly and authored a bill that established programs to provide meals for them as well. He was primarily responsible for the establishment of the House Committee on Aging. (The committee began operating in 1975 and Pepper became chairman in 1977.) He was the chief sponsor of five of the first National Institutes of Health and ten Alzheimer's Disease Research Centers. His 1978 bill, which abolished mandatory retirement at any age for federal government workers and raised from 65 to 70 the age at which nonfederal employees could be forced out of work, set the groundwork for the final step toward abolishment of mandatory retirement in 1986.

These are not the senator's only achievements on behalf of the elderly. The list would require an entire volume devoted to the topic. Suffice it to say that his efforts on behalf of older people have touched every area of their lives from housing to nutrition to health care. He is presently working for Congressional passage of a bill that would provide complete health coverage for everyone regardless of income.

At a recent talk at the National Press Club in Washington, D.C., Pepper was asked what philosophy keeps him going at age 88. His reply: "The philosophy of animation." He advises his peers: "Keep busy at the things that you like to do so that you can look back with satisfaction at what you did." If Claude Pepper ever stops long enough to look back, he undoubtedly will be able to see generations of older persons smiling back with thanks for the improved lives he has provided for them.

Art Buchwald Doesn't Like Being an Old Boy Wonder

America's favorite satirist expresses feelings similar to those most people have about aging: "I didn't like becoming 60. I was a boy wonder. And at 60 you can no longer call yourself a boy wonder." He adds: "I walk around now and people say to me 'You know when I was a *tiny* little girl I used to read you.' It's kind of sad. I don't think of myself as old until everyone tells me they read me when they were little."

With affection, columnist Art Buchwald had been called everything from a Jewish leprechaun to this century's Jonathan Swift. (Personally I think he looks like the cherub who runs the best delicatessen inside the pearly gates.) He is an American institution—friend to many a celebrity, foe of a president or two (Lyndon Johnson hated him). At 61, the Pulitzer Prize wimmer has a column syndicated in about 530 newspapers. He has a new book on thc shelves, *I Think I Don't Remember,* and he continues to make about forty or fifty speeches a year.

A typical Art Buchwald column will make fun of whomever is occupying the White House at the time, hence the title of his recent book, *While Reagan Slept.* Although Art has poked a great deal of fun at Ronald Reagan, he does say: "Ronald Reagan is a role model for anyone who is older because he looks great. Everybody likes him because he looks so great."

Clearly, to Buchwald, retirement is a dirty word. "I would never do that," he says as if you had just asked him to walk down Pennsylvania Avenue dressed in plastic wrap. His advice to those who may be considering retirement is: "Don't go to Florida. It speeds up the aging process. How much golf can you play?"

If Julia Child gets an A+ when it comes to planning ahead to make her older years positive years, Buchwald is in line for a conference with the homeroom teacher. Asked in 100 words or less to sum up his philosophy on aging, Art used six words: "Ignore it. It will go away." He adds: "The only thing to do is go with the flow. There isn't a damn thing you can do about it and if you are going to have to do an awful lot of things to grow older, I don't see that either. If you enjoy yourself, fine, but at some point in time you become a pain in the ass to everybody," he says. In other words, "Plan ahead? *Beeeyick.*"

When asked what he sees ahead for himself for the next ten years Buchwald says with a titter: "To continue my column—probably win the Nobel prize." He resists all attempts to pin him down further. When asked what he'll do after he wins the Nobel prize he replies: "Well then I'll probably just go around and get awards from everybody."

Buchwald expresses particular disdain when it comes to exercise. "I think exercise is dangerous. People should stay in the horizontal position as much as possible." His philosophy is: "When you get to this age you should enjoy yourself. If you want to exercise and do everything right—that's okay too. But if there's no fun enjoying it—the hell with it."

Art Buchwald's generous heart means that he is not a wealthy man. He gives a lot of money away and is a soft touch for benefits. Characteristically, he is sympathetic to the children of aging parents when the parents are problems. "This is the truth," he says, "the people who were not a pain in the ass when they were 40 and 50 are not a pain in the ass when they're older, but the ones who were really become ones then. They're guilt makers. A lot of guilt makers out there. Most kids feel so guilty about their parents." His advice to them is to join a club so that they will find out that everybody's having the same problems. "There should be groups that just meet to talk about their parents," he says.

Summing up his thoughts on older age Buchwald states: "A lot of people find today that they don't think in terms of age. You meet a friend and you're thrown because he's 70. You don't believe it because the way things are now, age is not as important as it used to be. The only thing that makes age important is whether they require you to resign or not."

Art Buchwald will never resign and he will keep us laughing while he collects every award imaginable, except maybe the Senior Olympics.

Part Two

Steps to Obtain a Long Life, Health, and Happiness

DID YOU KNOW?

Older is better.

The average age of the top Fortune 500 executives is 60.

One of the ironies of ageism—the prejudice toward older age—is that people become prejudiced against themselves.

Older age begins later than it used to and includes more healthy years.

Six out of ten people agree that life gets better as they get older.

One of the paradoxes of aging is that as more healthy years are added to life, so are more unhealthy years. Hence the need to plan ahead.

I never expected to have, in my sixties, the happiness that passed me by in my twenties. ***C.S. Lewis***

Your Positive Years

What does growing older mean? To Oliver Wendell Holmes it was the urge to call policemen "sonny." Henry Wadsworth Longfellow likened aging to opportunity. The opportunity to age is introduced at conception and encompasses a diverse span that is a study in contrasts—from the wonder of birth and infancy to the awkwardness of adolescence and the maturity of adulthood and older age.

The assumption that older age is a to-be-expected part of the life cycle is a gift of our times. Until this century, disease, the environment, and childbirth snuffed out the majority of lives by mid to late adulthood. Today most people live well into their 70s and beyond. In fact, since the beginning of this century, eight hours a day have been added to the average life span—25 years so far in this century.

This is a good time in which to be aging. Let's look at some facts about the role that older persons play today.

- The average age of our Supreme Court justices is 70.
- More than one-third of our state governors are over 55.
- Almost a fourth of US Representatives are over 60 as are almost a third of US Senators.
- The average age of today's top Fortune 500 executives is 60.

The list below shows you what a few famous older Americans were up to in the year this book was written. For example: 100-year-old George Abbott opened a play on Broadway; Norman Vincent Peale, 89, published his 34th book; and four popular TV shows, "Dynasty," "The Golden Girls," "Murder, She Wrote," and "Matlock" starred popular actors and actresses over 60.

These policy makers, authors, and stars are carrying on a tradition begun in ancient times, when many of the classic greats did their best work after age 60. On winning the Kentucky Derby at 54, Billy Shoemaker summed up the attitude that enables these individuals to continue their accomplishments beyond what is usually thought of as normal retirement age: "When you think you're old, you act old. My problem, I guess, is that I don't think I'm old." Bob Hope says virtually the same thing: "Everybody asks me how come I can still work and dance at my age and I say it's very simple . . . don't act your age."

Watch Out for Ageism

The Bob Hopes and Billy Shoemakers of the world are making their older years prime time years. Unfortunately, for some, older age is based on a prejudice Pulitzer prize winning author Robert Butler calls "ageism"—prejudice toward older people. You may laugh, you may scoff, you may sigh. We have racism, sexism, and now ageism? Yes, it's ridiculous and, unfortunately, very real.

Ageism is manifested in our society's worship of youth and its anxiety over wrinkles, in the contradictions of our desire for longevity and reluctance to grow old, and in the media's use of phrases like "Geritol jock" (an aging athlete) and "era of the geezer" (Reagan's presidency). Ageism can occur at any age. When Eddie Mannix, an old-time executive at Warner Brothers, saw a screen test of 34-year-old Fred Astaire, he reportedly said: "He's too old and too bald."

Many people fall victim to ageism by ridiculously in older age becoming prejudiced against themselves. An episode of the "Mary Tyler Moore Show" reminded us of this when a delightful white-haired older man explained to perky, youthful Mary that part of his daily routine was going to a park and sitting on a bench. He found it rather boring, he said, but ever since he was little he had seen old men sitting on benches and felt it his obligation to the younger generation to do the same.

The moral of the story is clear: ageism can be a self-fulfilling prophecy. A child learns to expect old men to take to benches and, faithfully, in older age, sits out his expectation.

At 80 I believe that I am a far more cheerful person than I was at 20 or 30. I most deliberately would not want to be a teen-ager again. Youth definitely may be glorious but it is also painful to endure. Moreover, what is called youth is not youth, it is rather something like premature old age.

Henry Miller, on turning 80

A *New York Times* article about 12 fantastically successful elderly artists neatly describes the absurdity of prejudice toward older age. Painter Robert Motherwell, 71, had to deal with an all-too-common frustration for people of so-called retirement age at the engagement reception for his oldest daughter: "I was startled by how many people asked, 'Have you retired yet?' Then, "the idea of age became very vivid to me. For me, to retire from painting would be to retire from life." His unthinking guests had equated Motherwell's senior citizen status with a loss of ability to continue the creative process. This is ageism.

A *Christian Science Monitor* article by Lee Neville tells a favorite story about the pressures to act your age that are inherent in ageism:

> Walking down a residential street the other day, I came across an older woman playing hopscotch with a little girl. Fascinated, I stopped to watch. They seemed to be having so much fun. Besides thoroughly enjoying herself, the hopping woman showed considerably more vigor and agility than I, who must have been at least 10 years her junior. When the game was finished, the little girl clapped

> her hands. "I won. I won. But you always beat me, Grandma."
>
> The grandmother turned toward me, a twinkle in her eyes. "I haven't had so much fun since I tried to ride my youngest grandson's skateboard." Almost every day my daughter says to me, "Mama be your age." But I tell her, "I'll be any age I please. The nursing homes are full of old ladies being their age."

These stories remind us how ridiculous it is to stereotype older people into shriveled, wrinkled life positions because of chronological age. We need to stand back from ageism and take an earnest look at what aging means for us. None of us should assume that older age will be spent hand-in-hand with Ben-Gay, prune juice and a cane. At the same time, we need to avoid hiding behind the golden ages or best years labels that present a carefree image of aging that is equally unrealistic. In truth, older age does require some adjustments and it may bring problems.

If I had known when I was 21 that I should be as happy as I am now I should have been sincerely shocked. They promised me worm wood and the funeral raven.

Christopher Isherwood at age 70

Ageism's Self-Sabotage Checklist

One of the great lessons that psychology teaches us is that people behave, think, and feel, in large part, according to the feedback they get from their environment. Columnist Ellen Goodman explains the effect of this feedback on age this way: "At age 2 we are required to be terrible, at 6 to go to school, and by 65 or 70 at the latest to be old." The following checklist can help you determine whether you, perhaps through no fault of your own, impose the clock-work myths of ageism on yourself.

- Do you avoid doing things you'd like to do because you're afraid your age might make you feel out of place?
- Do you find yourself thinking things like, "I can't do that (start a new career, go dancing, take a vacation) because I'm too old?"
- Do you feel that it is inevitable that negative and extreme age-related changes will happen to you? Do you feel there is nothing you can do about these changes?
- Do you equate looking old with looking bad?
- Do you pretend to yourself or others that you're younger than you are?
- Do you find yourself feeling ashamed of physical signs of aging such as age spots and wrinkles?

We who are older have nothing to lose! We have everything to gain by living dangerously. We can be the risk takers, daring to challenge and change systems, policies, lifestyles, and ourselves. ***Maggie Kuhn***

- Do you find yourself avoiding the elderly or frail people in your life?
- Do you find yourself not wanting to think about older people because of your own fears (particularly if they are in places that make you uncomfortable, such as nursing homes or hospitals)?
- Do you feel that on issues such as employment or leadership you have few choices because of your age?
- When you hear that someone you are about to meet is over 75 do you assume that they're over the hill?

If you find yourself answering yes to any of these questions, you're guilty of shooting yourself in the foot with the bullets of ageism. If you answer yes to more than three you may be shooting yourself in *both* feet!

How to Tackle the Prejudice Against Older Age

If you are aging (we all are) and you dislike this fact, *it's probably not your fault*. This prejudice is deeply ingrained in our country's attitudes and advertising. But there are steps you can and should take to tackle ageism. Here are four of them.

First, *understand why it is important*. If you are older, you may sometimes be treated like a second class citizen. You may find yourself an object of prejudice. (If you are younger, you're next.)

Second, *shake ageism by its roots*—the fear of disease, of giving up youth, and, ultimately, of death. Fear of poor health and death is at the root of ageism. Woody Allen has this to say about our intrinsic fear of death: "I'm not afraid to die. I just don't want to be there when it happens." But he must be there, all of us must. When we as individuals are able to be honest about our fears of aging and death, we will have begun the demolition of our prejudices against older age.

Third, *learn the truth about aging*—the good news and the bad—and, most of all, how to adjust to the kinds of changes we face, both the inevitable and the possible.

Fourth, *act on this knowledge.* Knowledge only becomes powerful when it is joined with a verb. This does not mean that you need to wear "stamp out ageism" stickers on your lapel (although this can have its value). It does mean *act where you live,* with your family and friends, in your place of work, your place of worship, or on the golf course. If someone "compliments" you by saying, "You have such a young mind," you can respond with a glare and something like, "Don't my 60 (70, 80) years of experience count for anything?"

The Good News About Aging

Let's begin demolishing our fears about growing older by focusing on the positive. There is much good news about aging. For example:

- Older age begins later than it used to and it includes more healthy years.

- When health problems occur they are usually not life-threatening. Two out of three older persons view their health positively.
- Older age often brings the freedom to pick up and go when you want and gives you the time to pursue interests that you didn't have time for before.
- Older age provides women with greater assertiveness and men with greater expressiveness.
- For many older persons, income is adequate and stable.
- Many mental health problems burn themselves out by older age.
- Many people find their greatest happiness in middle age or later.
- Couples are free of the responsibilities of children after late middle age. They can meet their children again as friends.
- Sex and sexuality are more relaxed for couples in their later years due to freedom from fear of pregnancy.
- Older age brings possibilities for contributing to your community, your friends, your history, and your culture.

Many people develop new confidence and pride in their older years.

For her book *Pathfinders,* Gail Sheehy developed a life history questionnaire to "probe the self-perceptions, values, goals, coping styles and experiences at each stage of life of adults between the ages of 18 and 80." She sent the questionnaire to 60,000 people, published it in *Redbook* and *Esquire,* and then did a series of personal interviews based on the questionnaire. She found that those who had the greatest sense of well-being were likely to be older. In Sheehy's words: "Older is better."

Sheehy found older women to be the most satisfied. In fact, middle-aged women went off the chart in happiness. In general, for women, life satisfaction generally rises through the mid-50s and at age 57 it takes off and soars. Says Sheehy: "Between the mid-50s and 65, the issue of trying too hard to please is surmounted for the first time. Women begin at last to value themselves."

The pattern for men is different. Men tend to hit a low point in their early 50s, but reach high satisfaction in their late 50s. Happiness then rises in the early part of the 60s and, for a considerable number, levels off beyond that on a high plateau. Among the 1,200 members of the American Bar Association who Sheehy interviewed, for example, the most content men were those over age 65.

Many studies have shown that most older persons enjoy their later years. Researcher Bernice Neugarten, a leading gerontologist, reports very high levels of satisfaction among older persons. A classic study by Louis Harris Associates for the National Council on Aging (1981) found that almost 9 out of 10 people age 65 or older are "fairly well satisfied with their lives." More than half thought things seemed better in older age than they had anticipated they would be. (Life satisfaction in this group was heavily influenced by income and education.)

Louis Harris, reporting on happiness in his new book *Inside America,* says: "The older a person gets, the more satisfied he or she is with life. Only 53 percent of young people 18 to 24 express satisfaction. This rises to 73 percent among those 50 to 64, and levels out at 72 percent among those 65 and older."

For many years I have made it a habit when people ask me how I am to say loudly and enthusiastically: "I feel Healthy, I feel Happy, I feel TERRIFIC! As a result I never think of myself any other way. Today, at age 84, I feel healthier, happier, and more terrific each day than I did the day before.

W. Clement Stone

Two 1987 surveys confirmed these findings. A *USA Weekend Magazine* survey found that 6 out of 10 people of all ages agree that life gets better as they get older. The results also showed that, compared with younger people, those over 50 are happier than younger persons with their friendships, financial situations, marriages, or closest personal relationships. They also worry less. Another survey conducted by *USA Today* found that 6 out of 10 older persons like the age they are. Of the 65-plus respondents to the survey, 61 percent reported that they liked their present age. More than a third, 36 percent, said: "These are the best years" or "The best is yet to come."

More Good News About Aging: Fears vs. Facts

Many of the fears that you undoubtedly have about older age are based on myth. Will your physicist husband lose his brilliant mind? Will sex be but just distant memory? Will you end up in a nursing home? Compare feelings such as these with the realities of aging as shown below:

When you get older you will be unable to work.	Many studies show less absenteeism and fewer on-the-job accidents among older workers. They are *not* less efficient; they are more satisfied and report less stress than younger workers.
When you get older you will be sexless.	The majority of older Americans are sexually active.
When you get older you will be neglected by your children.	A national survey found that 81 percent of older persons with children reported having seen their children in the last week.
When you get older you will be isolated.	Nine out of 10 persons 65 or over who live by themselves manage to maintain social contacts. The majority live close to family members with whom they have frequent contact.

When you get older your memory will go and you will have trouble learning.	Although the ability to remember recent events sometimes becomes less acute, the learning and memory process *changes* (including slowing down) but does *not* become less effective. Older people can acquire new information and remember it as well as younger people.
When you get older your physical and mental health will decline.	While older people are prone to chronic ailments and do suffer some biological losses, they are less likely than younger people to have acute ailments. Dementias like Alzheimer's disease are the *exception* rather than the rule in older age, particularly for persons under 80.
When you get older you will end up in a nursing home.	Only 5 percent of older people live in nursing homes. In fact, more older people presently wear hearing aids than live in nursing homes.
You or your spouse may die soon after retirement.	There is *no* evidence for increased mortality after retirement.

As you can see many of the most common fears about older age are based on myth, not fact. Not only are these fears fiction, but older age as a chronological concept is itself obsolete.

Still More Good News About Growing Older: Older Age Starts Later Than It Used To

Today we're experiencing a blurring of the stages of life and the significance of age. Seventy-year-old mountain climbers and 50-year-old stroke victims are making chronological markers obsolete.

Bernice Neugarten refers to the blurring of age as "the fluid life cycle." She says: "All across adulthood, age has become a poor predictor of the timing of life events, as well as a poor predictor of a person's health, work status, family status, and, therefore, also, of a person's interests, preoccupations and needs."

When they can, gerontologists now like to define old age not by chronological age but by how well a person can function. Those older individuals who can no longer care for themselves are the OLD-OLD. They are separated from the YOUNG-OLD by frailty and the need for supportive services.

Forty is the old age of youth; fifty the youth of old age. ***Victor Hugo***

If one insists on putting an age bracket on the YOUNG-OLD years they generally last into the mid- to late-70s.

Most readers of this book are among the YOUNG-OLD for four out of five older persons are in this group.

What does all this mean to you? If you are like most older Americans today you can claim the compliment that you are younger than your years. Fifty is younger than it used to be, as are 60, 70, or 80. Today your so-called elderly years, if you experience them, will probably begin at about age 75, not at 65. This means that if you are 50 today you have another quarter-century before you will start showing significant signs of age. Even beyond 85 you may not be among the OLD-OLD. At age 85 two out of five people do not have to limit activity of any kind.

Yet we must be realistic. While older age can be better, it can also bring problems. This is one of the great paradoxes of life. With age come wisdom and contentment. But age also brings increased vulnerability to disease, some inevitable slowing, and loss of friends and loved ones. For example, while increased longevity translates into more healthy years, for many this is a mixed blessing because it can also mean more unhealthy years.

Preparation is the key. "You'd better plan for it," says Julia Child. "Prepare, not repair." says B. F. Skinner.

To be seventy years young is sometimes far more cheerful than to be forty years old.
Oliver Wendell Holmes

This is what some famous older Americans were up to in 1987.

GEORGE ABBOTT, 100, playwright, Pulitzer Prize winner: directing a revival of *Broadway* on Broadway

ELIZABETH "LIBBA" COTTEN, 95, Grammy Award winner, composer of "Freight Train": performing her folk blues music in Boston

ARTHUR MURRAY, 92, dancing master: dancing with his wife of 61 years at the Kahala Hilton in Honolulu every Saturday night

GEORGE BURNS, 91, actor, Oscar winner at age 80: continuing his stage act at Caesar's Palace in Las Vegas

LILLIAN GISH, 91, actress, who in her 80s danced and sang the boop-boop-a-doop song "I Wanna Be Loved By You" on Broadway: costarring in *The Whales of August* with Bette Davis

NORMAN VINCENT PEALE, 89, minister and author of *The Power of Positive Thinking,* one of the most influential works of our time: continuing as publisher of two magazines, *Guideposts* and *Plus,* and publishing his 34th book, *Power of the Plus Factor*

ARMAND HAMMER, 88, entrepreneur: running his multimillion dollar corporation, acting as unofficial goodwill ambassador between Washington, DC, and Moscow, and publishing his biography, *Hammer*

HELEN HAYES, 87, actress, two-time Oscar winner, author of *Our Best Years,* in which she offers such warm, personal views about growing older as: "What becomes fragile when we age is not our bodies as much as our egos.": publishing a new book on middle age

LOUISE NEVELSON, 87, sculptor: affirming that "I ain't through yet!" continues to work on her masterpieces

CARLETON E. MORSE, 85, creator of radio shows such as "One Man's Family" and "I Love a Mystery": publishing his first novel, *Killer at the Wheel*

JOHN HOUSEMAN, 84, actor, Oscar winner, former director of the Juilliard School's drama division: continuing his patrician advertisements for the investment firm of Smith Barney, and taking on such jobs as hosting a comedy show for NBC-TV

THEODORE SEUSS GEISEL, aka DR. SEUSS, 83, writer of children's books, Pulitzer Prize winner: continuing to head the *New York Times* bestseller list with his book for obsolete children, *You're Only Old Once*

JOSEPH COTTEN, 82, actor: publishing his autobiography, *Vanity Will Get You Somewhere*

ISAAC BASHEVIS SINGER, 82, writer, Nobel Prize winner: hard at work on a new book

AGNES DE MILLE, 81, dancer and choreographer, author (since her stroke some ten years ago, she has written three books): hard at work on a new book

JULES STYNE, 81, songwriter, composer of Peter Pan's "Never Never Land" and the music for *Gypsy, Funny Girl,* and *The Bells Are Ringing:*

hard at work writing the music for a new play, *Bar Mitzvah Boy*

JAMES MICHENER, 80, author of 32 books, Pulitzer Prize winner: published a short novel, *Legacy,* on the US Constitution, and working on a novel about the Caribbean

BETTE DAVIS, 79, actress, two-time Oscar winner: publishing her book *This 'n' That* and costarring in *The Whales of August* with Lillian Gish

REX HARRISON, 79, actor: considered returning to the stage in W. Somerset Maugham's *The Constant Wife*

MILTON BERLE, 78, comedian: appearing in the gala benefit "Show Business Applauds Lincoln Center"

ALISTAIR COOKE, 78, US citizen since 1941, best known in the United States as the host of "Masterpiece Theatre": continuing his BBC radio series "Letter from America" and celebrating his 2,000th broadcast

M. F. K. FISCHER, 78, writer: although unable to type because of Parkinson's disease, working on a new manuscript with a tape recorder

JESSICA TANDY, 78, actress: on location for the filming of *Cocoon II*

EUDORA WELTY, 76, writer, Pulitzer Prize winner: working on a new book

HUME CRONYN, 76, actor: on location for the filming of *Cocoon II*

RONALD REAGAN, 76, former actor, former governor, at age 69 the oldest United States president to ever be inaugurated: maintaining a busy schedule as president and physically hearty despite an assassination attempt, cancer surgery, his wife's mastectomy, and a fall in popularity due to the Iran-Contra affair

PERRY COMO, 75, singer: released his 73rd record album

SIR GEORGE SOLTI, 75, music director of the Chicago Symphony: picking up his 25th Grammy award

MARY McCARTHY, 75, author of 19 books: publishing the first volume of her autobiography and working on the second volume

ART LINKLETTER, 74, TV entertainer and author of *Kids Say the Darndest Things:* kicking off Senior Citizens Month in Appleton, Wisconsin, with the words: "Seniors say the darndest things—because they are free of the inhibitions of young people"; publishing a book on aging, *Old Age Is Not for Sissies*

JANE WYMAN, 73, actress, Oscar winner: starring in the prime time soap opera "Falcon Crest"

FRANK SINATRA, 72, singer: crooning at a concert at Verona's Rome Amphitheatre

PETER TAYLOR, 70, writer, winner of the Pulitzer and Ritz-Hemingway prizes: walking away with all of 1987's major literary awards for his second novel, *A Summons to Memphis*

OSSIE DAVIS, 70, actor: appearing in *I'm Not Rappaport* on Broadway

KATHERINE GRAHAM, 70, chairman of the board of the Washington Post Company: keeping up her busy schedule as head of one of the nation's top newspapers; receiving the esteemed Communication Award from the

Center for Communication for "uninterrupted courage and leadership and excellence in jounalism"

RAYMOND BURR, 70, actor: starring in the made-for-TV movie "Perry Mason: The Case of the Sinister Spirit"

JOHN FORSYTH, 69, actor: continuing his TV role as leading man in the hit series, "Dynasty"

ELLA FITGERALD, 69, jazz singer: continuing to delight audiences and winning a medal from UCLA for her musical achievements

ANN LANDERS, 69, columnist: claiming: "Retire? Who me? Surely you jest. I can't imagine anything less appealing": moving her popular daily column, "Dear Ann Landers," from the *Chicago Sun-Times* to the *Chicago Tribune*

MICKEY ROONEY, 67, legendary actor: planning to build 40 theaters across the country where people can go to see "old-fashioned" plays

STEVE ALLEN, 65, comedian, composer, pianist, author, originator of the "Tonight" show: publishing his 28th book and starting a new career in radio

SID CAESAR, 65, comedian: playing Frosch the jailer in *Die Fledermaus* at the Metropolitan Opera for eight performances

JIMMY AND ROSALYNN CARTER, 62 and 59, former president and first lady: publishing *Everything to Gain,* a call to action for bored retired persons

JASON ROBARDS, 64, actor, two-time Oscar winner: starring in *A Month of Sundays* on Broadway

CHARLTON HESTON, 64, actor, Academy Award winner: starred in the TV prime time soap opera "The Colbys"

JOSEPH HELLER, 63, author: at work on a sequel to *Catch 22*

BETTY WHITE, 63, and BEA ARTHUR, 61, actresses: starring in the TV sitcom "Golden Girls"

ANDY GRIFFITH, 61, actor: starring in the TV drama "Matlock"

Achievements from 70 to 100

At 100 Grandma Moses illustrated *'Twas the Night Before Christmas.*

At 93 George Bernard Shaw wrote the play *Far-Fetched Fables.*

At 90 Pablo Picasso was producing drawings and engravings.

At 90 Bertrand Russell intervened with heads of state during the Cuban missile crisis.

At 90 Duncan McLean won the 1975 World Veterans Olympic silver medal for the 200-meter run.

At 89 Artur Rubinstein gave one of his greatest recitals in Carnegie Hall.

At 87 Konrad Adenauer was chancellor of West Germany.

At 86 Arturo Toscanini was a vigorous conductor.

At 82 Winston Churchill wrote *A History of the English-Speaking Peoples.*

At 81 Benjamin Franklin effected the compromise that led to the adoption of the US Constitution.

At 81 Thomas Edison patented his last invention.

At 79 Marc Chagall produced two magnificent murals for the Metropolitan Opera in New York.

At 75 Duke Ellington made his last recording.

At 74 Claude Monet painted his famous water lilies.

At 71 Cecil B. De Mille produced and directed the award-winning *Greatest Show on Earth.*

At 71 Michelangelo was appointed chief architect of St. Peter's Basilica in Rome.

At 71 Charles Darwin published *The Power of Movement in Plants.*

At 70 Verdi finished *Falstaff.*

In his 70's Frank Lloyd Wright designed many of his masterpieces, including the Guggenheim Museum in New York.

In his 80s Titian was producing some of his finest works.

DID YOU KNOW?

One out of five Americans is 55 or older.

Average US life expectancy at birth is 75, 72 for males and 79 for females.

Beyond age 85 American women outnumber men five to two.

Most people are retired by age 65.

Age does not determine medical risk.

No one knows for sure why people age; anyone who tells you that aging has a specific cause is spouting theory, not truth.

No one ever dies of old age.

A man of sixty has spent twenty years in bed and over three years in eating.

Enoch Arnold Bennett

Aging in the Twentieth Century

If you are older you are a pioneer. As mentioned earlier, it is only in this century that older age has become an expected part of the life cycle. In 1900 *1* out of *20* Americans was over 50 and the average life expectancy was *47* years. A married couple could expect that one or the other would die before all of their children had left home. Today, *1* out of *5* Americans is 50-plus and our average life expectancy is *75* years. Now a husband and wife who are 60 can expect to reach 65 together.

The Aging of America

This is indeed the century of older age. In fact, there are now more Americans over 65 than there are teen-agers. Because of its permanent effects, the longevity revolution is having and will have far more impact on society than the birth and aging of the baby boom. While one out of five Americans today is over 55, by the year 2010 one out of four will be in this age group.

Let's look at some of the major trends that are part and parcel of the greying of our population. We're now a society in which the majority of Americans live to enjoy one to two decades of older age. But our lengthening life spans present some paradoxes. Older age means economic security for many, for example, but for others, who may have worked hard all their lives, it means poverty.

One aspect of aging in the twentieth century that is curious is the longevity advantage of older women. For instance, for those over 65, older women outnumber older men by three to two. This is why many gerontologists consider aging a woman's issue. If so, then not aging long enough should surely be a man's issue!

Here are some other important facts about aging today.

- ALMOST 70 PERCENT OF AMERICANS TODAY LIVE TO AGE 65 AND BEYOND.
  If you are 65 today and you are male, you can expect to live about another 15 years. If you are a woman you can expect to live another 19 years. (Don't forget these are averages; you may be on the short or long end of them.) Average life span is now 75 years. A baby boy born today could expect to live to age 72, while a baby girl could expect to live an additional seven years, to age 79.
- LONGEVITY MEANS MORE HEALTHY YEARS, BUT ALSO MORE UNHEALTHY YEARS.

One of the biggest dilemmas for health professionals and researchers studying aging is that while those who are part of the longevity revolution can expect to have more healthy years added to their lives, they also can expect more unhealthy years.

- DIVERSITY IS THE RULE IN OLDER AGE.
  As people get older, they become less alike and more heterogeneous. People tend to become exaggerations of themselves as they age, which accentuates individual differences. In other words, the stubborn become obstinate and the jokers become clowns.
- WEALTH AND INCOME VARY TREMENDOUSLY FOR OLDER PEOPLE.
  While some older people are very well off and others are part of a secure middle class, a surprising number have practically no economic resources. In recent years, there has been a growing perception that older people are doing quite well economically. While this is good news for many, this is not the case for large numbers of individuals. Widows, single women, the very old, and minorities are the most likely to have very low incomes.
- MOST PEOPLE ARE RETIRED BY AGE 65.
  Guesstimates are that at least two-thirds of today's retirees left work before age 65 at an average age of 61 years. People tend to leave work earlier for health reasons, because of the availability of private pensions, or because of lessening economic demands coupled with job

dissatisfaction. The fact that people tend to retire from full-time jobs before age 65 does not, however, mean that they prefer not to work. Three-fourths of the labor force would prefer to work part-time after retirement if they could.

- MOST MEN ARE MARRIED AND LIVE WITH A SPOUSE WHILE MOST WOMEN ARE WIDOWED, DIVORCED, OR SINGLE AND LIVE ALONE.
  In 1985, more than two-thirds of men over 75 and fewer than a fourth of women that age were living with spouses. These differences result from women's greater life expectancy and the fact that most married women are younger than their husbands.

- THE TRUE DEMOGRAPHIC REVOLUTION IS THE INCREASE IN THE VERY OLD.
  The survival of large numbers of people into their ninth decade is one of the major achievements of improved disease prevention and health care in this century. The number of Americans over 85 is expected to more than double from 2.2 million to 4.9 million between 1980 and 2000. And the number of 100-year-olds is expected to quadruple by the end of the century to 100,000 people.

- MOST OLDER PEOPLE ARE NOT SENILE.
  Mental impairment is the result of disease; it is *not* a normal part of the aging process. Fewer than 6 percent of all men and 3 percent of women over 65 are severely cognitively impaired. Alzheimer's disease is the leading cause of cognitive impairment.

- AGE IS NOT A MAJOR DETERMINANT OF MEDICAL RISK.
  For example, research shows that otherwise healthy older people are almost as likely as younger people to recover from open-heart surgery.

Old age is no such uncomfortable thing if one gives oneself up to it with good grace.

Horace Walpole

Research on Aging

What exactly is aging and what causes it? For example, why do houseflies live for only six weeks (thank God), humans for about 75 years, and turtles for over 100 years? Or why do women live, on average, seven years longer than men? Unfortunately, here our knowledge is limited. The study of biological aging and longevity is in the toddler stage.

Four hundred and fifty years ago Ponce de Leon began his futile search for the fountain of youth. Today's explorers—scientists in white lab coats supported by millions of federal dollars—are still trying to unlock time's secrets. Two of the biggest unanswered questions are why life has an upper limit and the location of the mainsprings of aging.

The upper limit on human longevity—the longest time anyone has ever lived—remains at about 115 years (and these cases are rare). And the limit is not advancing. The oldest documented person in the United States died in 1928 at age 115.

More important, we don't know how the aging process is controlled. We do know that the clocks of aging exist and that a combination of genetics controls aging's timing mechanisms, but the location of the mechanisms remains a mystery. Scientists are pursuing these mechanisms in DNA, other genetic material, the brain, hormones, and related biological components.

Researchers have developed various theories on why and how aging works. Because these theories are no more than sophisticated conjecture, no one should regard them as gospel. For example, the authors of the best-selling book *Life Extension* claim that there are two basic classes of aging mechanisms, one of which is "genetically programmed obsolescence." In truth, genetically programmed obsolescence is a *theory* and no more. It is, in fact, dangerous to assume that this theory is truth and to promote a health regimen based on it.

In general terms, the present theories on aging are:

- GENETIC PROGRAMMING, in which maturity, aging, and death follow a timetable similar to the timetable of early growth and development.
- DAMAGE TO VARIOUS BODY SYSTEMS THROUGHOUT LIFE due to factors such as wear and tear on the organism or harmful environment and foods.
- CHANGES IN BODY HORMONES such as those released by the pituitary gland. Release of a hormone or failure to produce one could cause aging to begin.

- WEAKENING OF THE IMMUNE SYSTEM, which is the body's mechanism for fighting disease. Weakening of the system opens the way for infection by viruses, bacteria, and other disease-producing organisms.

Principles of Aging

Four basic principles about the aging process are widely agreed upon by scientists studying aging. Most people are startled by the fourth principle: no one ever dies of old age. This does not mean that aging does not contribute to death. An older gentleman's reflexes might have slowed down to the extent that he could not get out of the way of an out-of-control truck, or his stiff arteries might make recovery from an acute disease episode impossible, but if he were to die it would be the truck or the acute episode that killed him—not old age.

Here are the principles:

- ALL INDIVIDUALS AGE AT DIFFERENT RATES.
  If you were to compare your own aging with that of another person born at the same exact time, there is only a very slight chance that you would have aged at exactly the same rate.
- AN INDIVIDUAL'S ORGANS DO NOT AGE AT THE SAME RATE.
  As Nathan Shock of the Gerontological Research Institute in Baltimore, Maryland puts it: "A 40-year-old man may have the heart of a 30-year-old but the liver of a man 10 or 20 years older."

Or you might like Jonathan Swift's description better: "I'm as old as my tongue and a little older than my teeth."

- THE LAST STAGES OF LIFE ARE DOMINATED BY THE BODY'S INABILITY TO RECOVER FROM STRESS AND TRAUMA.
  An 80-year-old woman running for a bus with a 30-year-old will take much longer to get her heart rate and breathing back to normal.
- WHILE OLD AGE EVENTUALLY ENDS IN DEATH AND THERE IS AN UPPER LIMIT TO LIFE SPAN, NO ONE DIES FROM OLD AGE.
  In other words, you will eventually die from a heart attack, an accident, or some other unfortunate episode, but you will not just die of old age.

Aging Research Is an Optimistic Science

Clearly, there is still much to be learned about age and aging. The basic philosophy that underlies all of aging research, however, is well-established. Aging is an optimistic science that, at the present time, focuses on adding quality to longer lives. It is to our nation's credit that we have increased funding continually for such optimistic research primarily through the National Institute on Aging, one of the National Institutes of Health.

An important advance that has been made in the study of aging is the identification of the factors that are needed for a long, happy, healthy life. Taking Control of the Aging Process takes a detailed look at these factors.

Gerontology will not abolish old age; it will make it happen later . . . old age itself will not be longer, only later. ***Alex Comfort***

Through the Decades

1910 Taft is president and war threatens. The tango is the rage; women wear full-length tight skirts and high button shoes. The first movie made in Hollywood is a year away. The Model T costs $825, and the average annual earnings of a full-time employee are $517. Over 50 percent of all American males age 10 to 15 years are full-time bread winners. There are 92 million Americans. One in 10 is age 55 or older and 1 in 25 is age 65 or older. The death rate for persons age 55 to 64 is 56 per 1,000. A baby boy born this year has a life expectancy of 50 years. A little girl has a life expectancy of 54 years. The average length of time in retirement for males is 1 year.

1920 President Wilson is on the way out and Harding is coming in. Bobbed hair is the rage and skirts are worn calf-length. Prosperity abounds. The number of women workers increases, and regularly scheduled radio broadcasts begin. The divorce rate is 1.6 per 1,000 Americans. Eighty-six out of 1000 infants die before seeing their first birthday. Life expectancy at birth for males has increased by five years since 1910 to 55 years. Life expectancy at birth for females has increased by two years to 56 years.

1930 The stock market had crashed, the Great Depression is on, and Hoover is president. The first "talkie" had been released two years earlier. Movie theaters interrupt their screenings to broadcast "Amos and Andy." Art Deco prevails, and permanent waves replace bobbed hair. There are 123 million Americans. The public debt is $16,185,309,831 or $131.51 per capita. Life expectancy for those who reach age 65 is 12 years for men and 13 years for women.

1940 President Franklin Delano Roosevelt is in his seventh year of office. The movie *Gone With the Wind* had been released a year earlier and the Swing Era is at its peak. Americans turn to their radios to listen to Jack Benny and for news of the war, while Nazi forces invade Denmark, Belgium, Holland, Norway, and Luxembourg. The next year, 1941, would see 672 people per 100,000 die from the measles. The Social Security Act had been passed in 1935 and 147,000 persons age 65 or older are now receiving monthly checks from the Social Security Administration. The average check is $36.40. Life expectancy at birth is 61 for males and 66 for females. Retirement is now an institution; the average length of time in retirement for males is ten years.

1950 Harry Truman is president. The Golden Age of TV begins. Red Fever is rampant; people move to the suburbs in droves, and flying a commercial liner across the Atlantic is now common. Women wear well-tailored slacks, for sportswear only. There are 151 million Americans. The death rate for infants has dropped to 30 per 1,000. The typical American family has two parents, three children, and the mother stays home to raise the children. Life expectancy at birth is 66 for males and 71 for females.

1960 Dwight David Eisenhower is president. The peak of the baby boom has just passed and the walls of America's schools are bulging. The longest economic boom on record is just beginning. "The Twist" is the rage; bouffant hairdos double the size of ladies' heads, and the average American TV set is now on six hours a day. The average annual earnings of a full-time employee are $4743. The death rate for people age 65 to 74 has dropped to 38 per 1,000. Life expectancy for men and women is now seven years apart, 67 years for males and 74 years for females. (The gap in life expectancy would close a little again to five years difference for men and women in 1970 and then it would widen again.)

1970 Richard Milhous Nixon is president. Medicare and Medicaid had become law five years earlier. The Viet Nam war resistance heightens and pantsuits and mini-skirts are in. The Beatles are culminating careers as the most successful group in the history of popular music. There are now 203 million Americans, and 17,571,000 people 65 or older are receiving monthly checks from the Social Security Administration. The average check is $198.90. Twenty-three people per 100,000 die of the measles. Life expectancy for males has advanced by 21 years since the beginning of the century, from 46 in 1900 to 67 in 1970. For females, 26 years have been added to life, from a life expectancy of 49 in 1900 to 75 in 1970.

1980 Jimmy Carter is voted out of office and Ronald Reagan is voted in. The night time TV soap opera "Dallas" is at the height of its record-breaking popularity. A 1980 Ford Thunderbird costs over $12,000. The divorce rate is 5 per 1000 Americans; one half of all marriages now end in divorce. There is no typical American family—the rule is diversity in family forms. Life expectancy at age 65 is 14 years for men and 18 years for women. The average length of time in retirement for males is now 14 years.

1985 Ronald Reagan is in his second term of office. The movie *Cocoon,* whose stars are in their 70s, is a hit and string bikinis are in. There are 237 million Americans. Aging has become a major public policy issue. One in five Americans is now age 55 or older and one in eight is age 65 or older. Over half of all mothers with children work; terrorism is on the rise, and the public debt is $1,823,103,000,000 or $7,614.51 per capita. Life expectancy at birth is 71 for males and 78 for females.

Aging in the Twenty-First Century: An Interview with John Rother

John Rother, director of research and public policy for the American Association of Retired Persons (AARP), is one of the major figures working in the field of aging today. In the fall of 1986 he was asked to look toward the next century and give us some predictions on aging in the year 2000 and beyond. Rother sees a world in which older people have more choices, but, unfortunately, more limitations as well. He also prepares us for a two-tiered older population of haves and have-nots.

Here is Rother's view of what's ahead. The trends he describes will shape and be shaped by today's baby-boom and older generations.

The Top Ten Trends in Aging for the Twenty-First Century

1. THE MATURE CULTURE. The Census Bureau predicts that by 2010 one out of four Americans will be age 55 or older. The sheer strength of numbers will mean that older persons will dominate America's cultural, political, and commercial systems. The youth culture will be replaced by a mature culture that will reflect the values associated with maturity—such as humor, wisdom, commitment, monogamy, and the importance of leaving a legacy.
2. A CONFUSING ENVIRONMENT. Today's PPOs, HMOs, SHMOs and so on are just the start of a blossoming of diverse organizational forms. Older people will be able to take advantage of a wide range of programs for everything from political action to weight loss to health care. The plethora of choices will make the environment much more diverse and baffling, but there will also be much more opportunity to match people up with the right choice. Entire new service industries will spring up to explain,

recommend, or match peoples' needs with the full range of options.

3. THE "SENIOR LEAGUE." Because the older population is becoming increasingly more educated and income and health status are rising, there will be more resources available in the twenty-first century than at present. Older people who are active will replace the wife/homemaker as the volunteer mainstay of most communities. Instead of the junior league we'll have a senior league as more and more communities turn to seniors for help in meeting local needs.

4. OLDER SEX OBJECTS AND POWER BROKERS. The media will finally catch on to the rich diversity among the older generation and the tendency to stereotype older people into declining, doddy grandparents will decline. We can see this beginning to happen now, in the late eighties, with the "Golden Girls," the grandparents on the "Bill Cosby Show," and John Forsyth's character on "Dynasty."

   In the future we'll see more public portrayals of older people in every imaginable capacity—from power broker to sex object. An actor's age will no longer be a primary limitation on the roles he or she can play. This will have important consequences as public attitudes about appropriate behavior for older people are eased.

5. TECHNOLOGY FOR THE ISOLATED. Today there is a strong trend toward older people

living by themselves. For instance, today about half of all women age 75 or older live alone. This trend will continue, making it harder for those who are isolated to reach out or be reached. However, technology will provide a friendlier, more accessible environment for those living alone such as shopping by TV, electronic mail, telephone counseling, and emergency response systems.

6. A CHOICE OF FAMILY TIES. With a higher divorce and remarriage rate than ever before, millions of children will reach adulthood with several sets of grandparents. At the same time, due to the high numbers of women who are not and will not bear children, millions of retirement age individuals will have no "blood" grandchildren. The result will be that the legal, financial, and emotional obligations that go with family identity will be much more complex—to the point where we will choose which relatives we will keep up "family ties" with, and which people, not necessarily related by blood or marriage, will constitute a functional family.

7. MORE JOB OPPORTUNITIES. As fewer of the baby bust younger generation (who were born in smaller numbers after the baby boom) enter the labor force, employers will offer more flexibility in jobs in order to attract and retain older employees. There will be more opportunities for those who want to work.

8. INCREASED DISABILITY. The greatest irony of today's health care advances is that they succeed in keeping us alive longer, but not necessarily in better functional health for all of those added years. In the future people with disabilities living in the community will be much more prevalent than we can imagine today. There will be two major responses to the increased number of people with disabilities. The focus of medical care will necessarily shift from acute care to chronic care. And we will be pushed in our families, our communities, and our nation to support caregiving for the chronically ill and disabled.

9. SELF-HELP GROUPS. One of our great American traditions is self-help—in which participants learn from those who have been there before or tackle a challenge with the support of others who share the same goal. As the population ages the self-help trend will surge, for everything from volunteer safe driving groups to exercise and weight loss programs to education to politics.

10. GREATER INEQUALITY. One unplanned consequence of a society with greater choices over a lifetime is greater inequality. Choices imply the right to make poor decisions, uninformed decisions, or decisions for immediate goals at the expense of retirement goals. Three choices in particular—the choice of a marriage partner, the choice of a state to reside in, and the choice of employer(s) will have a major

impact on individuals' circumstances as they age in the twenty-first century.

A stable, enduring marriage is not a requirement for successful aging. Most anyone spending their retirement years alone can attest to the fact that it does help tremendously, however. In addition, living in a locality with an adequate tax base and the will to support services for the elderly can make the difference between maintaining independence in the community or institutionalization during extreme older age. And the same is true for employment where an adequate inflation-adjusted pension is earned, and even more important, health benefits are covered in retirement. Unfortunately, these factors, along with others, will create a two-tier retirement population: a first tier of comfortable and secure Americans, for whom our system has worked well to assure that the "golden years" live up to their name and a second tier of those who get left behind compared to the rising prosperity around them.

A key public policy question for the twenty-first century will be the extent to which we allow the consequences of a lifetime of greater choices to develop into a society of winners and losers as each generation nears the finish line. The shape of public policy will have to change to be more concerned with those likely to be on the bottom tier. Let's hope that is a smaller group than those in need today.

DID YOU KNOW?

A 50-year-old man or woman today who keeps risk factors low can expect to live 11 years longer than his or her contemporaries who do not follow such approaches.

Eighty percent of all premature deaths could be avoided through health prevention techniques, accident prevention, and more careful medical care.

Quit smoking, and even after 40 years of smoking 2½ packs a day, your lungs will go back to near normal.

A recent study found that men who exercised off 2,000 calories a week had a 28 percent lower death rate than less active men.

Having a stressed personality takes three years off of normal life expectancy.

Drinking two cocktails, beers, or glasses of wine a day takes one year off of normal life expectancy.

Successful aging requires an active decision. That decision can be made at 20 or 30 or at 40 or at 60 or at 70. It doesn't make a whole lot of difference when that decision is made, but adapting to old age is an active process, and you have got to decide that you will adapt actively to it, rather than have the years overcome you passively. **Eric Pfeiffer**

Taking Control of the Aging Process

There are specific steps that you can take to add years to life and, more important, add health and happiness to your extra years. No, sorry, there are no quick fixes, no known life extenders or anti-aging treatments that prolong life or slow aging. Anyone who offers to sell you XYZ hormones or r2b2 pollens to live longer is offering to sell you bunk.

The Need to Actively Adapt

It is true, however, that specific personal practices *which are under your control* can greatly increase your chances of living longer while being healthier and happier. Incorporating these practices into your lifestyle means *taking control of the aging process before it takes control of you*. For example, according to work done at the Carter Institute under the direction of Bill Foege, a 50-year-old man or woman today who keeps risk factors low can expect to live 11 years longer than contemporaries who don't follow such approaches.

Before we discuss the steps to longevity, health, and happiness (which are basically common-sense practices), let's talk about the three principles that make them work: acceptance, attitude, and action.

Acceptance

Make peace with the fact that you are growing older. According to George H. Pollock, director of Chicago's Institute for Psychoanalysis, "The people who cannot accept that they are no longer 25 or 39 are the ones who have trouble getting older." Learn about the aging process and about the factors that lead to a healthy and happy longer life. In other words, make a conscious decision to *take control of the aging process.*

If your birthday candles would overwhelm a 12-inch cake, yet you are physically young and vigorous, *taking control* may simply mean keeping up a healthy routine of good nutrition, exercise, and activity. If you feel emotionally bruised by the loss of a loved one, and if time has not eased the depression, *taking control* may mean seeking professional help or attending a self-help group in order to work through the grief. Or, if you have a disabling condition such as advanced arthritis, *taking control* may mean accepting the limitations posed by the disease; carrying on a healthy routine of good nutrition, exercise, and activity; and using "capability aids" such as tub seats and grab bars when needed.

In other words, *taking control* means being realistic about your age, viewing it positively, and actively managing any problems related to it.

It's not how old I am, it's how I'm old.
Groucho Marx

Attitude

Noted gerontologist James Birren sums up the importance of attitude in this way: "We now realize that the way we feel, think and behave influences how long we're going to live." This is the theme underlying the popular self-help movement of the eighties, which addresses such problems as substance abuse, nervous disorders, overweight, and recovery from grief. We are what we think and do. If you *act old,* others will treat you as if you're old, and you, in turn, will *think old.*

Interpretation is everything. Pessimists experience down-and-out old ages. Optimists experience up-and-at-'em old ages. This happens regardless of how frequently death has stolen away loved ones, regardless of the presence or absence of disease, regardless of how much money is in the bank. Attitude alone can make the difference between a healthy, positive longevity or a shorter, negative life.

The National Institute on Aging emphasizes the importance of a positive attitude in its public service materials called "Can Anything Be Done To Extend Life?": "It helps to have a positive attitude toward life. EXPECT to live a long time. Plan ahead for housing and financial security. Find out what makes you happy and do it."

If you know that you are capable of a negative attitude which, like a perpetual sore tooth, gets in the way of the enjoyment of life, you might also be thinking, "But, I'm too old to change." Hogwash. Judith Viorst, in *Necessary Losses,* talks about the fact that attitude and personality can change at any age: ". . . changes are possible, even unto the seventh, eighth, ninth decade. We are never a 'finished product'—we refine and we rearrange and we revise . . . We can change in old age because every stage of our life, including our last one, affords new opportunity for change." In other words, no one is too old to shape up his or her attitude.

You're only old once. **Dr. Seuss**

Action

After we accept the need to adapt actively to older age and shape up our attitude, it's time for *action.* This means actively doing the things that are known to be effective for adding healthy, happy years to life.

A Dozen or So Common-Sense Steps to Long Life, Health, and Happiness

J. Michael McGinnis, deputy assistant secretary for health, disease prevention, and health promotion at the US Department of Health and Human Services (HHS), relates a startling finding: Only 20 percent of premature deaths—those that occur earlier than the national average—are due to heredity. In fact, *80 percent of all premature deaths could be avoided through health prevention techniques, accident prevention, and more careful medical care.*

> Quit smoking and, even after 40 years of smoking two and a half packs a day, your lungs will go back to near normal.

2. EAT A BALANCED DIET AND MAINTAIN YOUR DESIRED WEIGHT. Good diet and nutrition can actually prevent the development and progression of disease in later life. According to nutritionist Marianna Cadigan:

   > There is ample evidence in medical and research literature to indicate that the nutritional status and nutrition behavior of an individual are directly related to health and longevity.

   Diet is strongly related to heart disease, cancer, and stroke. This is particularly important to you, as an older person, because you have a three out of four chance of dying from one of these three diseases. Also, if physical problems, accidents, or illness occur, and you have had a good nutritional history, your chance of recovery will be much greater. Research studies also demonstrate that the well-nourished body is better able to tolerate chemotherapy and surgery if either is ever needed. According to experts, however, most of the older population is at nutritional risk. In other words, to reverse a popular phrase, most older persons are *not* eating right to keep fit. *Resolve not to be among them.*

   > Although there is considerable controversy over the question of whether being under-

weight aids longevity, it is clear that even slight obesity is unhealthy. Ten to 30 pounds of overweight takes two years off of normal life expectancy. Thirty to 50 pounds of overweight takes off four years, and over 50 pounds takes off eight years. New studies indicate that for many obese people, relatively small weight losses can correct problems such as a tendency toward diabetes.

3. EXERCISE REGULARLY. Pulitzer Prize winning geriatric psychiatrist and former director of the National Institute on Aging Robert Butler says: "If exercise could be packed into a pill, it would be the single most widely prescribed, and beneficial, medicine in the nation."

   Exercise does not have to mean jogging or aerobic dancing. Even moderate exercise has tremendous benefits. A recent study directed by Ralph S. Paffenberger, Jr., a researcher at Stanford University School of Medicine and the Harvard School of Public Health, found that men who exercised off 2,000 calories a week had a 28 percent lower death rate than less active men. The benefits of regular exercise are so numerous they would fill a book thick enough to allow a three-year-old grandchild to see over the edge of your dining room table. And yet 60 percent of males and 65 percent of females over 65 do not exercise regularly.

   Many of the benefits of exercise are listed in the second volume of *Prime Time*. For the sake of emphasis, however, let's briefly recite some of the most important here. People who exercise regularly recover more quickly from medical interventions, have stronger hearts and lungs, have lower blood pressure, and are protected against the start of adult-onset diabetes. Exercise strengthens bones, slows down the progress of osteoporosis, strengthens and tones muscles, and helps you move about more easily by keeping joints, tendons, and ligaments flexible. Exercise also gives you more energy, helps you sleep better and feel less tense, and contributes to mental health. Don't take it easy—exercise!

> Working out every day or working at a job that requires regular, vigorous activity adds three years to normal life expectancy. Inactivity—not getting much exercise at home, at work, or for recreation—takes three years off of normal life expectancy.

4. HAVE REGULAR HEALTH CHECK-UPS, SEE A HEALTH PROFESSIONAL WHEN YOU DETECT A PROBLEM, AND FOLLOW A DOCTOR'S ADVICE WHEN TAKING MEDICATIONS. As you grow older, it is important to locate health professionals who are knowledgeable about and sensitive to the health problems that can occur during older age. For instance, many doctors still assume that memory loss is a natural part of the aging process. *It is not.*

   Most doctors recommend annual check-ups by a physician after age 55 unless you are at risk for a specific problem that requires more frequent monitoring. The National Institute on Aging recommends that older Americans see a dentist every year and have a complete eye exam every two or three years.

The worst thing about growing old is listening to the children's advice. **Anonymous**

---

5. STAY INVOLVED WITH FAMILY AND FRIENDS. Samuel Silverman, a Harvard University psychiatrist, says you can add up to 15 years to your life by reducing loneliness and another emotional factor, repressed anger. Having a strong "convoy" of social support—a number of close relationships, family, and friends to contribute help to and draw help from when needed—gives its members a feeling of self-worth. The value of a convoy has been borne out by research. For example, loss of caregivers rather than physical deterioration precipitates nursing home placement. And, in a study of 3,000 Iowans over 65, researchers found that the loneliest are five times as likely to be institutionalized and four times more likely to die than those who are not lonely.

   There is not only safety in numbers; one close friendship can provide a special emotional cushion in times of crisis. Remember your "blood" brother or sister? Remember that special little boy or girl you proudly called your best friend? Best friends are as important at 55 or 80 as they were at five or eight. It is important to have one confidant with whom you can share the ups and downs of your life.

BEWARE: If you are an older person who is isolated, you are probably continuing a lifelong pattern. It is important that you overcome your social reticence in order to ward off the negative psychological effects of social isolation.

I find friendship to be like wine, raw when new, ripened with age, the true old man's milk and restorative cordial. ***Thomas Jefferson***

---

6. ALLOW TIME FOR REST AND RELAXATION. Anthropological studies have shown that stress ages people more quickly. Stress has a number of physiological effects such as pushing up levels of "bad" cholesterol, raising blood pressure, and altering body chemistry.

   Having a stressed personality—with traits of aggression, ambition, and nervousness (such as having sleepless nights or biting your fingernails)—takes three years off of normal life expectancy.

The amount of sleep required by the average person is just fifteen minutes more.

Anonymous

---

7. GET ENOUGH SLEEP. You should get enough sleep every 24-hour period to feel rested. During the later years it is common to wake often during the night and sleep less at nighttime. Therefore it is important to find other ways of getting the amount of rest your body requires. There's nothing wrong with a cat nap in the mid-morning or afternoon.

   You should, at the same time, guard against sleeping too much. Sleeping over seven to eight hours a day can be a sign that something is wrong. Consult a physician if you are sleeping too much.

   > Sleeping more than ten hours a night is equated with a life expectancy that is four years shorter than normal.

Growing old is no more than a bad habit which a busy man has no time to form.

André Maurois

---

8. STAY ACTIVE THROUGH WORK, RECREATION, AND COMMUNITY ACTIVITIES. Gerontologists agree that the people who do best in older age are the ones who plan ahead and stay busy. Consider what Julia Child has to say: ". . . lead as active and productive a life as you can all the time. You're lucky if what you like falls upon you, otherwise you will just have to find it . . . If you sit around doing nothing your mind will go foul. I've noticed it myself, if you're

too busy and you've got all sorts of schedules, you don't get sick."

I'm a bit tired but I am well. I've completely finished Otello! ***Verdi at age 73***

Working past retirement age or being so active that you do not have time to do all the things you want adds three years to normal life expectancy.

9. DRINK ALCOHOLIC BEVERAGES IN MODERATION, IF AT ALL, AND DON'T DRIVE AFTER DRINKING. Alcohol and drug abuse are on the rise for all age groups. Overuse of alcohol poisons the body with severe effects, from irreparable liver damage to memory loss. Miriam Stoppard, author of *The Best Years of Your Life,* warns that moderate to heavy drinking has a cumulative negative effect on the body. According to Dr. Stoppard:

   As we grow older, our central nervous systems undergo progressive change, and with this change comes an alteration in our tolerance of alcohol. The toxins that have been accumulating in our bodies reach a level that is damaging to our systems. Changes in our central nervous system can cause a dramatic change in our level of tolerance for alcohol. The person who could drink several beers and still feel fine when he was young and active may find, as he grows older, that even a single drink will have a definitive effect on his ability to function.

> Drinking two cocktails, beers, or glasses of wine a day takes one year off of normal life expectancy. For each additional drink per day, two years are subtracted. Not drinking adds two years to normal life expectancy.

One martini is all right, two is too many and three is not enough. **James Thurber**

---

10. USE SEAT BELTS. In the next ten years of normal driving, it is almost certain that you will be involved in a motor vehicle accident serious enough to injure or even kill you, according to the US Department of Transportation. Motor vehicle accidents are a major public health concern. On average, almost 900 people die each week in traffic accidents and another 10,000 are injured every day.

    According to the National Institute on Aging, research shows that older drivers have a higher accident rate per mile than younger drivers and are more likely to be injured or killed when in an accident due to more fragile bones and a reduced ability to withstand trauma. The simplest and most effective way to protect yourself is to fasten your seat belt.

11. AVOID OVEREXPOSURE TO THE SUN AND COLD. With age, the body is less able to respond to heat or cold. Overexposure to both can be fatal. Hot or humid weather can cause hyperthermia, heat stroke, or exhaustion, especially if you have heart and circulatory disease, are susceptible to stroke, or are diabetic. Symptoms are faintness, dizziness, headache, nausea, loss of consciousness, rapid pulse, and flushed skin.

    Cold weather can lead to hypothermia, a drop in internal body temperature. Symptoms are a slowed heartbeat and breathing, slurred speech, sluggishness, and confusion.

    Stay warm in winter, cool in summer.

The diseases which destroy a man are no less natural than the instincts which preserve him.

Georges Santayana

---

12. PRACTICE GOOD SAFETY HABITS AT HOME TO PREVENT ACCIDENTS SUCH AS FIRES AND FALLS. As an older person, you are in the highest risk group for accidents of any age group. Accidental injuries occur with more frequency and are more serious in later life. Recovery is also much slower. Falls are the most common form of injury for older people. Accident proof your home and watch your step.

13. KNOW YOUR FAMILY HISTORY AND TAKE MEASURES TO REDUCE RISKS. This last recommendation does not come from the National Institute on Aging, but is the author's. The tendency to develop many diseases runs in families. There are specific things that can be done to stave off inherited diseases and physical problems. If you have a history of cancer in your family, find out what the American Cancer Society recommends and carry it out. If you are at risk for arthritis, follow the advice of the Arthritis Foundation, and so on.

Keys to Well-Being

In addition to the keys to health and longevity just described, other important practices lead to well-being during older age. Here are some of them.

Money: a guarantee that we may have what we want in the future. Though we need nothing at the moment, it insures the possibility of satisfying a necessary desire when it arrives. ***Aristotle***

- FINANCIAL KNOWLEDGE. Protect your retirement income by being informed about money matters such as Social Security, Medicare, pensions, and tax benefits for older Americans. For example, most older people do not realize that *if the need strikes, Medicare does not cover long-term nursing home or home-health care.* (This has not been changed under new government provisions for catastrophic care.) Too many discover the impact of this public policy failure when a long-term illness strikes and they have nowhere to turn. There is a flip side to this issue. Those older people who do know of Medicare's inadequacy are a prime market for useless insurance policies that claim to, but do not, offer supplemental coverage to Medicare. Be informed.

- ABILITY TO DEAL WITH BUREAUCRACIES. If details make you want to tear your hair out, you'd better plan now for how you are going to camouflage the bald spots on your head after you reach Social Security age. As an older person, you will have to deal with the bureaucracies that oversee such programs as Medicare, Social Security, pension plans, or private health insurance, to mention but a few. These bureaucracies are notorious for taking potentially simple tasks and making them as tortuous as possible. People who plan ahead and allow themselves ample time to deal with the paperwork these bureaucracies require or who seek professional assistance do better.

Pride is the sworn enemy of content.
Thomas Fuller

- ABILITY TO COMPENSATE FOR SENSORY FAILURES. This practice has been aptly described by B. F. Skinner in his book *Enjoy Old Age.* You will not necessarily be afflicted with sensory failures in your senior years. But if they do occur don't let false pride keep you deaf, unstable, or doubtful. If you have trouble hearing normal conversation, don't be ashamed to wear a hearing aid. If your memory is getting rusty, use tricks such as: a place for everything and everything in its place.

You're not crippled at all unless your mind is in a splint. **Frank Scully**

- ABILITY TO COMPENSATE FOR PHYSICAL PROBLEMS. As you age, independent living may require some adjustments to your home environment. Often these adjustments make the difference between at-home and institutional living. If you have trouble standing to take a shower, which is a common problem for people with specific disorders or of very advanced aged, get a tub seat. If you have trouble climbing stairs and the entrance to your home is up two flights, install a ramp. If you can't reach your kitchen sink, have it, and all your counter tops, lowered (if you can afford it).

Appendix One

Places to Go for Help

These addresses are relevant to all five volumes of *Prime Time.* If you feel that you need guidance on a specific problem or if you want to volunteer your time, these national organizations can help you or put you in touch with the right organization for you.

Federal and Private Agencies on Aging

American Association of Retired Persons (AARP)

AARP is by far the best known of the aging organizations. It has 29 million members 50 and over and more than 3,000 chapters across the country. Services include: political advocacy on health care and other issues, consumer and driving improvement programs, and a wide variety of informative publications. AARP also sells insurance and travel services and has a mail-order pharmacy.

AARP
1909 K St. NW
Washington DC 20049
(202) 872-4700

Gerontological Society of America (GSA)
GSA is an association of professionals in the multidisciplinary field of aging.

Gerontological Society of America
Suite 300
1411 K St. NW
Washington DC 20005
(202) 393-1411

Grey Panthers
The Gray Panthers work to change laws and attitudes that discriminate against older people.

Grey Panthers
Suite 601
311 S. Juniper St.
Philadelphia, PA 19107
(215) 545-6555

National Association of Area Agencies on Aging (N4A)
N4A represents the 600 Area Agencies on Aging across the country (see the following section of this appendix).

(N4A)
Suite 208 W
600 Maryland Ave. SW
Washington DC 20024
(202) 484-7520

National Council on the Aging (NCOA)

NCOA is a membership organization that primarily serves professionals working with the elderly, but also offers some services to individuals.

National Council on the Aging
West Wing 100
600 Maryland Ave. SW
Washington DC 20024
(202) 479-1200

National Council of Senior Citizens (NCSC)

NCSC is a political advocate group for older persons and, through its 400 clubs across the country, offers a variety of services.

National Council of Senior Citizens
925 15th St. NW
Washington DC 20005
(202) 347-8800

National Institute on Aging (NIA)

NIA is a federal research agency that is part of the National Institutes of Health. It offer a series of informative publications including *Age Pages*.

National Institute on Aging
Public Information Office
Room 5C35, Building 31
9000 Rockville Pike
Bethesda, MD 20205
(301) 496-1752

The Older Women's League (OWL)

OWL serves the needs of older women and lobbies for issues of importance to them. OWL has 96 chapters in 36 states.

The Older Women's League
1325 G St. NW, Lower Level B
Washington DC 20005
(202) 783-6686

Apendix Two

State and Area Agencies on Aging

More than 600 State and Area Agencies on Aging cover every city and town in the United States with a variety of federally-funded services. Services that might be included in your area are senior centers, home-care workers, transportation, counseling, meal programs, and information and referral. The Area Agency on Aging closest to your area is the first place to call to find local services. The names and locations for all State and Area Agencies are listed here by state.*

*Reprinted with permission of the National Association of Area Agencies On Aging, Inc.

ALABAMA

(Federal Region IV)

STATE AGENCY ON AGING

Oscar D. Tucker, Executive Director
COMMISSION ON AGING
502 Washington Avenue
Montgomery, Alabama 36130
(205) 261-5743

AREA AGENCIES

PSA	Area agency address	Director and telephone number
1	Northwest Council of Local Governments Area Agency on Aging, P.O. Box L, 438 S.W. Hamilton St., Russellville, Ala. 35653.	Mr. Elliott Conway ....(205) 332-9173
2	West Alabama Planning and Development Commission, 7601 Robert Cardinal Airport Rd., Tuscaloosa, Ala. 35406.	Ms. Pam McDaniel ....(205) 345-5545
3	Birmingham Regional Planning Commission, 2112 South 11th Ave., Suite 220, Birmingham, Ala. 35205.	Ms. Mary Lou Rasco ....(205) 251-8139
3a	Jefferson County Office of Senior Citizens' Activities, 2601 Highland Avenue, South Birmingham, Ala. 35205.	Ms. Barbara Bonfield ......(205) 251-2992
4	East Alabama Regional Planning and Development Commission, P.O. Box 2186, 1130 Quintard Avenue, Anniston, Ala. 36202.	Mr. Porter Benefield ....(205) 237-6741
5	South Central Alabama Development Commission, 3968 Governors Drive, P.O. Box 20028, Montgomery, Ala. 36111.	Ms. Sylvia Alexander ......(205) 281-2196
6	Alabama Tombigbee Regional Commission, P.O. Box 269, Camden, Ala. 36726.	Ms. Janice Armstrong .....(205) 682-4234

7	Southeast Alabama Regional Planning and Development Commission, P.O. Drawer 1886, Dothan, Ala. 36302.	Mr. William Glover	(205) 793–0446
8	Area Agency on Aging—South Alabama Regional Planning Commission, 250 N. Waterstreet, P.O. Box 1665, Mobile, Ala. 36601.	Ms. Joan States	(205) 433–6541
9	Central Alabama Aging Consortium, 818 S. Perry, Suite 1, Montgomery, Ala. 36104.	Ms. Mavis Hicks	(205) 265–8320
10	Lee County Area Council of Governments, 118 N. Ross St., P.O. Box 1072, Auburn, Ala. 36830.	Ms. Gayle Boswell	(205) 821–3042
11	North Central Alabama Regional Council of Governments, 402 Lee St. NE., P.O. Box C, Decatur, Ala. 35602.	Mr. Norris Turney	(205) 355–4515
12	Top of Alabama Regional Council of Governments, 115 Washington St., SE, Huntsville, Ala. 35801.	Ms. Nancy Robertson	(205) 533–3330

ALASKA*

(Federal Region X)

STATE AGENCY ON AGING

OLDER ALASKANS COMMISSION
Department of Administration
Pouch C-Mail Station 0209
Juneau, Alaska 99811–0209
(907) 465–3250

*The State of Alaska serves as a single planning and service area.

ARIZONA

(Federal Region IX)

STATE AGENCY ON AGING

Michael Slattery, Director
AGING AND ADULT ADMINISTRATION
Department of Economic Security
1400 West Washington Street
Phoenix, Arizona 85007
(602) 255-3596

AREA AGENCIES

PSA	Area agency address	Director and telephone number
1	Region 1 Area Agency on Aging, 1366 East Thomas Rd., Suite 108, Phoenix, Ariz. 85016.	Ms. Ruth Houghton . . . .(602) 264-2255
2	Pima Council on Aging, 2955 E. Broadway, Tucson, Ariz. 85701.	Ms. Marian Lupu . . . .(602) 795-5800
3	Northern Arizona Council of Governments, 119 East Aspen, P.O. Box 57, Flagstaff, Ariz. 86002.	Ms. Louise Wolverton . . . . . .(602) 774-1895
4	District IV Council of Governments, Area Agency on Aging, 1100 South Maple Avenue, Yuma, Ariz. 85364.	Ms. Joyce Verschoor . . . .(602) 782-1886
5	Pinal/Gila Council for Senior Citizens, Area Agency on Aging, 512 East Butte Ave., Florence, Ariz. 85232.	Mr. Richard Romero . . . .(602) 868-5400
6	Southeastern Arizona Governments Organization, SEAGO Area Agency on Aging, 118 Arizona Street. P.O. Box 204, Bisbee, Ariz. 85603.	Ms. Kathleen Heard . . . .(602) 432-5301

7	Navajo Nation Area Agency on Aging, Division of Health Improvements Aging Department, P.O. Drawer 1390, Window Rock, Ariz. 86515.	Mr. Stanley Benally	(602) 871–4941
8	Inter Tribal Council of Arizona, Inc., 124 West Thomas Rd., No. 201, Phoenix, Ariz. 85013.	Mr. John Lewis	(602) 248–0071

*PSA 8 includes all tribal reservations, except the Navajo Nation, and therefore has no beneficial boundaries.

ARKANSAS

(Federal Region VI)

STATE AGENCY ON AGING

Herb Sanderson, Director
DIVISION OF AGING AND ADULT SERVICES
Department of Social and Rehabilitative Services
Donaghey Building, Suite 1428
7th and Main Streets
Little Rock, Arkansas 72201
(501) 371–2441

AREA AGENCIES

PSA	Area agency address	Director and telephone number
1	Northwest Arkansas Area Agency on Aging, 910 Hwy 65 North, Northvale Shopping Ctr., P.O. Box 1795, Harrison, Ark. 72601.	Mr. Lloyd Kennedy . . . . (501) 741–1144 1–(800) 432–9721
2	White River Area Agency on Aging, P.O. Box 2637, 617 Virginia Dr., Batesville, Ark. 72501.	Mr. Thomas Lose . . . . (501) 793–4431
3	East Arkansas Area Agency on Aging, 311 South Main, P.O. Box 5035, Jonesboro, Ark. 72403.	Mr. Ed Doman . . . . (501) 972-5980 1–(800) 382–3265
4	Southeast Arkansas Area Agency on Aging, 115 E. 5th St., Suite 301, Pine Bluff, Ark. 71611.	Ms. Betty Bradshaw . . . . (501) 534–3268 1–(800) 272–2025
5	Central Arkansas Area Agency on Aging, P.O. Box 5988, 706 West 4th St., North Little Rock, Ark. 72119.	Ms. Dixie Clark . . . . (501) 758-2294 1–(800) 482–6359

6	West Central Arkansas Area Agency on Aging, 624 Malvern Ave., Hot Springs, Ark. 71901.	Mr. Darrell Smith	(501) 321-2811 1-(800) 272-2138
7	Southwest Arkansas Area Agency on Aging, 811 Calhoun Dr. P.O. Box 26, Magnolia, Ark. 71753.	Mr. David Sneed	(501) 234-7410
8	Western Arkansas Area Agency on Aging, P.O. Box 1724, 1411 Rogers Ave., Fort Smith, Ark. 72902.	Mr. Jim Medley	(501) 783-4500

CALIFORNIA

(Federal Region IX)

STATE AGENCY ON AGING

Alice Gonzales, Director
DEPARTMENT OF AGING
1600 K Street
Sacramento, California 95814
(916) 322–5290

AREA AGENCIES

PSA	Area agency address	Director and telephone number
1	Area 1 Agency on Aging, 3300 Glenwood St., Eureka, Calif. 95501.	Ms. Patty Berg . . . .(707) 442–3763
2	Area Agency on Aging, P.O. Box 1400, 228 Butte St. Yreka, Calif. 96097	Ms. Susan Davenport . . . . . .(916) 842–1687
3	PSA 3 Area Agency on Aging, California State University, Chico, Calif. 95929.	Mr. Paul Martinson . . . .(916) 895–5961
4	Area 4 Agency on Aging, 2862 Arden Way, suite 101, Sacramento, Calif. 95825.	Ms. Deanna Lee . . . .(916) 447–7063
5	Marin County Area Agency on Aging, Civic Center, room 257, San Rafael, Calif. 94903.	Ms. Ellen Caufield . . . .(415) 499–7396
6	San Francisco City and County Commission on Aging, 25 Van Ness St. Suite 650, San Francisco, Calif. 94103.	Ms. Joyce Ream . . . .(415) 557–5844
7	Contra Costa County Office on Aging, 2425 Bisso Lane, suite 110, Concord, Calif. 94520.	Mr. Carl Cole . . . .(415) 671–4233

8	San Mateo Area Agency on Aging, 617 Hamilton St., Redwood City, Calif. 94063.	Mr. Keith Shirasawa	(415) 363-4511
9	Alameda County Department on Aging, 1231 E. 11th St. Suite 207, San Leandro, Calif. 94578.	Ms. Barbara Helmuth	(415) 874-7233
10	Council on Aging of Santa Clara County, Inc., 2131 The Alameda, San Jose, Calif. 95126.	Mr. Stephen M. Schmoll	(408) 296-8290
11	San Joaquin County Area Agency on Aging, room 402, 222 East Weber Ave., Stockton, Calif. 95202.	Ms. Charlotte Humphrey	(209) 944-2448
12	Central Sierra Area Agency on Aging, 56 North Washington St., Sonora, Calif. 95370.	Mr. Michael Sirrine	(209) 532-6272
13	Seniors Council of Santa Cruz and San Benito Counties, Inc., 234 Santa Cruz Ave., Aptos, Calif. 95003.	Ms. Jennifer Davis	(408) 688-0400
14	Fresno-Madera Area Agency on Aging, 1221 Fulton Mall, suite 553, Fresno, Calif. 93721.	Ms. Barbara Pontecorvo	(209) 455-3278
15	Kings-Tulare Area Agency on Aging, 1920 West Princeton Drive, suite A and B, Visalia, Calif. 93277.	Mr. John Davis	(209) 733-1079
16	Inyo-Mono Area Agency on Aging, P.O. Box 1799, Bishop, Calif. 93514.	Mr. Charles Broten	(714) 873-4248
17	Central Coast Commission for Senior Citizens, 122C West El Camino, Santa Maria, Calif. 93454.	Ms. Joyce Lippman	(805) 925-9554
18	Ventura County Area Agency on Aging, 505 Poli St., 3rd Floor. Ventura, Calif. 93001.	Ms. Colleen House	(805) 654-3660
19	Los Angeles County Department of Senior Citizens Affairs, 1102 Crenshaw Blvd., Los Angeles, Calif. 90019.	Ms. Lynn Bayer	(213) 857-6403
20	Office of Aging, 686 E. Mill St., San Bernardino, Calif. 92415.	Ms. Kay Pichette	(714) 387-2423
21	County of Riverside Office on Aging, On the Mall at 6th Street, P.O. Box 1480, Riverside, Calif. 92502.	Mr. Terrence Loughran	(714) 683-7880
22	County of Orange Area Agency on Aging, 1300 S. Grand Ave. Bldg. B., Santa Ana, Calif. 92701.	Ms. Peggy Weatherspoon	(714) 834-6017
23	San Diego County Area Agency on Aging, 4161 Marlborough Ave., San Diego, Calif. 92105.	Mr. Daniel L. Laver	(714) 560-2427

CALIFORNIA—Continued

PSA	Area agency address	Director and telephone number
24	Imperial County Area Agency on Aging, 654 Main St., El Centro, Calif. 92243.	Mr. Richard Ramirez . . . .(619) 352–8521
25	Los Angeles City Department of Aging, 600 South Spring St. #900, Los Angeles, Calif. 90019.	Mr. Dennis Jackson . . . .(213) 485–4685
26	Mendocino-Lake Area Agency on Aging, 413A N. Lake St., Ukiah, Calif. 95482.	Ms. Andrea Lerned . . . .(707) 462–1954
27	Sonoma County Area Agency on Aging, 940 Hopper Ave., Santa Rosa, Calif. 95403.	Ms. Robin Schaef . . . .(707) 527–3138
28	Solano/Napa Area Agency on Aging, 1814 Capitol St., Vallejo, Calif. 94590.	Mr. Jack Cunningham . . . . . .(707) 644–6612
29	El Dorado County Area Agency on Aging, 937 Spring Street, Placerville, Calif. 95667.	Mr. Doug Nowka . . . .(916) 626–2149
30	Stanislaus County Area Agency on Aging, 1024 J St., room 416, Modesto, Calif. 95354.	Ms. Lynda Wood Shelton . . .(209) 526–6700
31	Merced County Area Agency on Aging Programs, 2150 M St., suite 3, Merced, Calif. 95340.	Mr. Dennis Tatum . . . .(209) 385–7550
32	Area Agency on Aging, 1184 Monroe St. #10, Salinas, Calif. 93906.	Ms. Vicki Shepard . . . .(408) 449–1877
33	Kern County Office on Aging, 1415 Truxton Ave., suite AB, Bakersfield, Calif. 93301.	Mr. Eddie Laine . . . .(805) 861–2445

COLORADO

(Federal Region VIII)

STATE AGENCY ON AGING

William Hanna, Director
AGING AND ADULT SERVICES DIVISION
Department of Social Services
717 17th St.
P.O. Box 181000
Denver, Colorado 80218-0899
(303) 294–5913

AREA AGENCIES

PSA	Area agency address	Director and telephone number
1	Northeastern Colorado Area Agency on Aging, 300 Main St., Fort Morgan, Colo. 80701.	Mr. Larry Alflen . . . . (303) 867–9409
2A	Larimer County Area Agency on Aging, Department of Human Development, P.O. Box 1190, 525 W. Oak St., Fort Collins, Colo. 80521.	Ms. Susan Pedersen . . . . (303) 221–7440
2B	Weld County Area Agency on Aging, Weld County Health Department Building, 1516 Hospital Rd., Greeley, Colo. 80631.	Ms. Linda Piper . . . . (303) 744–1573
3	DRCOG Area Agency on Aging, 2480 West 26th Ave., suite 200B Denver, Colo. 80211.	Ms. Susan Cockings-Aldridge (303) 455–1000
4	PACG/Council of Governments, 27 Vermijo St., Colorado Springs, Color. 80903.	Ms. Valerie Barber . . . . (303) 471–7080

5	East Central Area Agency on Aging, 535 Main St., Box 28, Stratton, Colo. 80836.	Ms. Liz Whipple	(303) 348–5562
6	Lower Arkansas Valley Area Agency on Aging, Ottero County Courthouse, P.O. Box 494, La Junta, Colo. 81050.	Ms. Lynn Graves	(303) 384–8165
7A	Pueblo Area Agency on Aging, #1 City Hall Pueblo Place, Pueblo, Colo. 81003.	Ms. Jane Fugate	(303) 544–4307
8	S. Central Colorado Seniors Inc., P.O. Box 896, Alamosa, Colo. 81101.	Mr. Bill Baker	(303) 589–4511
9	San Juan Basin Area Agency on Aging, Southwest Community Resources, 649 Sixth Street, Durango, Colo. 81301.	Mr. Charles Speno	(303) 259–1967
10	District X Regional Planning Commission, 301-B N. Cascade, Drawer 849, Montrose, Colo. 81402.	Mr. Stan Broome	(303) 249–2436
11	Associated Governments of Northwest Colorado, 202 Railroad Ave., P.O. Box 351, Rifle, Colo. 81650.	Mr. David Norman	(303) 625–1723
12	Skyline Six Area Agency on Aging, 409 Main Street, Suite 209,Box 739, Frisco, Colo. 80443.	Ms. Barbara Kienholz	(303) 668–5445
13	Upper Arkansas Area Agency on Aging, 1310 East Rainbow Blvd., No. 17, Salida, Colo. 81201.	Ms. Virginia Bedford	(303) 275–8350
14	Huerfano/Las Animas Area Agency on Aging, Council of Governments, room 201, Courthouse, Trinidad, Colo. 81082.	Mr. Walter Degurse	(303) 846–4401

CONNECTICUT

(Federal Region I)

STATE AGENCY ON AGING

Mary Ellen Klinck, Executive Director
DEPARTMENT ON AGING
175 Main Street
Hartford, Connecticut 06106
(203) 566-3238

AREA AGENCIES

PSA	Area agency address	Director and telephone number
1	Southwestern Connecticut Area Agency, 276 Park Ave., Bridgeport, Conn. 06604.	Ms. Edith Serke ....(203) 333-9288
2	South Central Connecticut Area Agency on Aging, 201 Noble St., West Haven Conn. 06516.	Ms. Carolyn Forbes ....(203) 933-5431
3	Eastern Connecticut Area Agency on Aging, 116 Franklin Street, room 219, Norwich, Conn. 06360.	Ms. Adele Tousignant ......(203) 887-3561
4	North Central Area Agency on Aging, 999 Asylum Ave., Hartford, Conn. 06105.	Ms. Maureen Mohyde ......(203) 278-2044
5	Western Area Agency on Aging, 233 Mill St., P.O. Box 820, Waterbury, Conn. 06722.	Mr. Larry March ....(203) 597-0442

DELAWARE

(Federal Region III)

STATE AGENCY ON AGING

Eleanor Cain, Director
DIVISION ON AGING
Department of Health and Social Services
1901 North DuPont Highway
New Castle, Delaware 19720
(302) 421–6791

*Serves as single planning and service area for State of Delaware.

DISTRICT OF COLUMBIA*

(Federal Region III)

D.C. Office on Aging

Veronica Pace, Executive Director
OFFICE ON AGING
1424 K. St. N.W.
2nd Floor
Washington, D.C. 20011
(202) 724–5626

*The District of Columbia serves as a single planning and service area.

FLORIDA

(Federal Region IV)

STATE AGENCY ON AGING

Margaret Lynn Duggar, Director
PROGRAM OFFICE OF AGING AND ADULT SERVICES
Department of Health and Rehabilitation Services
1317 Winewood Boulevard
Tallahassee, Florida 32301
(904) 488–8922

AREA AGENCIES

PSA	Area agency address	Director and telephone number
1	Northwest Florida Area Agency on Aging, 24 W. Chase St., suite A. Pensacola, Fla. 32501.	Mr. Mike Freeman ....(904) 436–5224
2	Area Agency on Aging of North Florida, 2639 North Monroe St., suite 145B, Box 12, Tallahassee, Fla. 32303.	Ms. Anne Menard ....(904) 488–0055
3	Mid-Florida Area Agency on Aging, 5700 S.W. 34th St., suite 222, Gainesville, Fla. 32608.	Mr. Dean R. LaFrentz ......(904) 378–6649
4	Northeast Florida Area Agency on Aging, 2722 College St., P.O. Box 43187, Jacksonville, Fla. 32205.	Ms. Elizabeth Lee ....(904) 388–6495
5	Tampa Bay Regional Planning Council, 9455 Koger Blvd., St. Petersburg, Fla. 33702.	Ms. Sally Gronda..........(813) 577–5151

6	Manahill Area Agency on Aging, 8405 North Himes Ave., suite 106, Tampa, Fla. 33614.	Ms. Maureen Kelly	(813) 933–5945
7	East Central Florida Area Agency on Aging, 1011 Wymore Rd., room 105, Winter Park, Fla. 32789.	Ms. Judith G. Thames	(305) 645–3339
8	Area Agency on Aging, 1402-02 Jackson St., Fort Myers, Fla. 33901.	Mr. William K. Clark	(813) 332–4233
10	Area Agency on Aging of Broward County, 5345 NW 35th Ave., Ft. Lauderdale, Fla. 33309.	Ms. Edith Lederberg	(305) 485–6370
11	Area Agency on Aging, Dade and Monroe Counties, 902 Southwest 2nd Ave., Miami, Fla. 33131.	Mr. Paul Hunt	(305) 579–2257

GEORGIA

(Federal Region IV)

STATE AGENCY ON AGING

Fred McGinnis, Director
OFFICE OF AGING
878 Peachtree Street, N.E.
Room 632
Atlanta, Georgia 30309
(404) 894–5333

AREA AGENCIES

PSA	Area agency address	Director and telephone number
1	Altamaha Georgia Area Planning and Development Commission, 505 W. Parker St., P.O. Box 328, Baxley, Ga. 31513.	Ms. Gail Thompson . . . .(912) 367–3648
2	Atlanta Regional Commission, 100 Edgewood Ave., NW., suite 1801, Atlanta, Ga. 30305.	Ms. Cheryl Schram . . . .(404)656–7767
3	Central Savannah River Area Planning and Development Commission, 2123 Wrightsbond Rd., P.O. Box 2800, Augusta, Ga. 30904.	Ms. Jennette Cumming . . . . .(404) 737–1823
4	Chattahoochee Flint Area Planning and Development Commission, 6 Shenandoah Blvd., Box 2308, Newman, Ga. 30264.	Mr. Bobby Buchanan . . . . . .(404) 253–8521
5	Coastal Area Planning and Development Commission, 127 F Street, P.O. Box 1917, Brunswick, Ga. 31521.	Mr. Myron Dice . . . .(912) 264–7363
6	South Georgia Area Planning and Development Commission, 327 W. Savannah Ave., P.O. Box 1223, Valdosta, Ga. 31601.	Ms. Maria Hill . . . .(912) 333–5277

7	Coosa Valley Area Planning and Development Commission, 1 Jackson Hill, P.O. Drawer H, Rome, Ga. 30161.	Ms. Ola Ayers	(404) 295-6485
8	Georgia Mountains Area Planning and Development Commission, 1010 Ridge Rd., P.O. Box 1720, Gainesville, Ga. 30501.	Ms. Pat Viles	(404) 536-3431
9	Heart of Georgia Council on Aging, 118 S. Second Ave., P.O. Box 503, McRae, Ga. 31055.	Mr. Murray Ward	(912) 868-5917
10	Lower Chattahoochee Area Planning and Development Commission, 930 S. Second St., P.O. Box 1908, Columbus, Ga. 31901.	Ms. Katie Carmack	(404) 324-4221
11	McIntosh Trail Area Planning and Development Commission, 408 Thomaston St., P.O. Drawer A, Barnesville, Ga. 30204.	Mr. Lanier Boatwright	(404) 358-3647
12	Middle Flint Area Planning and Development Commission, 203 E. College St., P.O. Box 6, Ellaville, Ga. 31806.	Mr. Mickey Holloway	(912) 937-2561
13	Middle Georgia Area Planning and Development Commission, 600 Grand Bldg., Macon, Ga. 31201.	Ms. Sylvia Haslem	(912) 751-6160
14	North Georgia Area Planning and Development Commission, 503 West Waugh St., Dalton, Ga. 30720.	Mr. Lawrence Besel	(404) 272-2300
15	Northeast Georgia Planning and Development Commission, 305 Research Rd., Athens, Ga. 30610.	Ms. Angela Rouse	(404) 548-3141
16	Oconee Area Planning and Development Commission, 3014 Heritage Rd., P.O. Box 707, Milledgeville, Ga. 31601.	Ms. Melinda Edwards	(912) 453-5327
17	SOWEGA Council on Aging, 309 Pine Avenue, P.O. Box 3149, Albany, Ga. 31701.	Ms. Kay H. Hind	(912) 432-1124
18	Southeast Georgia Planning and Development Commission, 3243 Harris Rd., P.O. Box 2049, Waycross, Ga. 31501.	Ms. Linda Carroll	(912) 285-6096

HAWAII

(Federal Region IX)

Jeanette Takamura, Director
EXECUTIVE OFFICE ON AGING
Office of the Governor
335 Merchant St.
Room 241
Honolulu, Hawaii 96813
(808) 548-2593

AREA AGENCIES

PSA	Area agency address	Director and telephone number
1	Kauai County Office of Elderly Affairs, 4396 Rice St., Lihue, Hawaii 96766.	Ms. Eleanor Lloyd ....(808) 245-4737
2	Elderly Affairs Division, Office of Human Resources, 650 South King St., Honolulu Municipal Bldg., Honolulu, Hawaii 96813.	Ms. Lynette Burns ....(808) 523-4361
3	Maui County Committee on Aging, 200 South High St., Wailuku, Hawaii 96793.	Mr. Roy S. Fusato ....(808) 244-7837
4	Hawaii County Office of Aging, 34 Rainbow Dr., Hilo, Hawaii 96720.	Mr. William Takaba ....(808) 961-3794

IDAHO

(Federal Region X)

STATE AGENCY ON AGING

Charlene Martindale, Director
OFFICE ON AGING
Room 114 – Statehouse
Boise, Idaho 83720
(208) 334–3833

AREA AGENCIES

PSA	Area agency address	Director and telephone number	
1	AID, 3655 North Government Way, #6, Coeur D'Alene, Idaho 83814.	Ms. Suzanne Reichelderfer	(208) 772–4096
2	Area II Agency on Aging, 1424 Main St., Lewiston, Idaho 83501.	Ms. Sharon Shrum	(208) 743–5580
3	Ida-Ore Planning and Development Association, 25 N. Idaho, P.O. Box 311, Weiser, Idaho 83672.	Mr. Elwin Grout	(208) 549–2411
4	College of South Idaho, 315 Falls Ave., P.O. Box 1238, Twin Falls, Idaho 83301.	Mr. Richard Boyd	(208) 733–9554
5	Southeast Idaho Council of Governments, 1070 Hilene Rd., suite 390, Pocatello, Idaho 83201.	Sr. Anthony Marie Greving	(208) 233–4032
6	East Idaho Special Services, 450 J Street, P.O. Box 1098, Idaho Falls, Idaho 83401.	Ms. Fran Schobield	(208) 522–5391

ILLINOIS

(Federal Region V)

STATE AGENCY ON AGING

Janet S. Otwell, Director
DEPARTMENT ON AGING
421 East Capitol Avenue
Springfield, Illinois 62701
(217) 785-2870

AREA AGENCIES

PSA	Area agency address	Director and telephone number
1	Northwestern Illinois Area Agency on Aging, 4223 East State St., Rockford, Ill. 61108.	Ms. Janet B. Ellis . . . .(815) 226-4901
2	Region II Area Agency on Aging, Community College W. Campus, Bldg. #5, P.O. Box 809, Kankakee, Ill. 60901.	Mr. Charles Johnson . . . .(815) 939-0727
3	Western Illinois Area Agency on Aging, 729 31st Ave., Rock Island, Ill. 61201.	Ms. Greta Brooks . . . .(309) 793-6800
4	Central Illinois Agency on Aging, 700 Hamilton Blvd., Peoria, Ill. 61603.	Ms. Barbara Miller . . . .(309) 674-2071
5	East Central Illinois Area Agency on Aging, RR 12, Box 16/1003 Maple Hill Rd, Bloomington, Ill. 61701.	Ms. Phyllis Pinkerton, ...(309) 829-2065
6	West Central Illinois, Area VI, Area Agency on Aging, P.O. Box 428, 1125 Hampshire St., Quincy, Ill. 62306.	Ms. Lynn Niewohner . . . . . .(217) 223-7904

7	Project Life Area Agency on Aging, 2815 West Washington St., suite 220, Springfield, Ill. 62702.	Ms. Dorothy Kimball	(217) 787-9234
8	Southwestern Illinois Agency on Aging, 333 Salem Place, Suite 225, Fairview Heights, Ill. 62008.	Mr. William Keel	(618) 632-1323
9	Midland Area Agency on Aging, Shawnee Rd., P.O. Box 1420, Centralia, Ill. 62801.	Ms. Deborah Kuiken	(618) 532-1853
10	Southeastern Illinois Area Agency on Aging, 302 Market St., Mount Carmel, Ill. 62863.	Mr. Harold Morris	(618) 262-8001
11	Egyptian Area Agency on Aging, 108 South Division St., Carterville, Ill. 62918.	Mr. George Everingham	(618) 985-8311
12	Department on Aging and Disability, 510 N. Peshtigo Ct., 3rd floor, Chicago, Ill. 60611.	Mr. Robert J. Ahrens	(312) 744-5775
13	Suburban Cook County Area Agency on Aging, 600 West Jackson, Suite 700, Chicago, Ill. 60606.	Mr. Jonathan Lavin	(312) 559-0616

INDIANA

(Federal Region V)

State Agency on Aging

Jean Merritt, Executive Director
DEPARTMENT OF AGING AND COMMUNITY SERVICES
251 North Illinois Street
P.O. Box 7083
Indianapolis, Indiana 46207–7083
(317) 232–7006

AREA AGENCIES

PSA	Area agency address	Director and telephone number
1	Lake County Economic Opportunity Council, Inc., 5518 Calumet Ave., Hammond, Ind. 46320.	Ms. Marianne Holmer ......(219) 937–3500
2	Area 2 Council on Aging, REAL Services, 622 N. Michigan St., P.O. Box 1835, South Bend, Ind. 46634.	Mr. James Oleksak ....(219) 233–8205
3	Northeast Area 3 Council on Aging, 5720 St. Joe Rd., Ft. Wayne, Ind. 46835.	Ms. Diann Chappell ....(219) 485–4026 (800) 552–3662
4	Area 4 Agency on Aging and Community Services, Inc., 10 N. Earl Ave., P.O. Box 4727, Lafayette, Ind. 47903.	Ms. Fay B. Ebrite ....(317) 447–7683 (800) 382–7556
5	Area 5 Council on Aging & Community Services, 912 E. Market St., Logansport, Ind. 46947.	Mr. Michael Meagher ......(219) 722–4451
6	Area 6 Council on Aging, 1968 W. Main St., Muncie, Ind. 47303.	Ms. Karen Gardner ....(317) 289–1121

7	West Central Indiana Economic Development District, 1718 Wabash, P.O. Box 359, Terre Haute, Ind. 47808.	Ms. Edna Faulk	(812) 238–1561 (800) 742–0804
8	Central Indiana Council on Aging, 615 N. Alabama St., suite 336, Indianapolis, Ind. 46204.	Mr. Duane Etienne	(317) 633–6191
9	Area 9 Agency on Aging, Indiana University East, 303 South A St., Richmond, Ind. 47374.	Mr. Tony Shepherd	(317) 966–1795
10	Area 10 Agency on Aging, 2129 Yost Avenue, Bloomington, Ind. 47401.	Ms. Jewel Eichelbarger	(812) 334–1769
11	Area 11 Agency on Aging, 4340 Jonathon Moore Pike, P.O. Box 904, Columbus, Ind. 47202.	Ms. Diane Cantrell	(812) 343–4992
12	Area 12 Council on Aging, P.O. Box 97, Dillsboro, Ind. 47018.	Ms. Sally Dobson	(812) 432–5215
13A	Area 13A Council on Aging, Vincennes University, P.O. Box 314, Vincennes, Ind. 47591.	Ms. Anne Jacoby	(812) 885–4292
13B	Southwest Indiana Council on Aging, 7–11 SE 7th Street, Evansville, Ind. 47708.	Mr. Robert Patrow	(812) 464–7800
14	South Central Council on Aging and Aged, 134 E. Main, New Albany, Ind. 47150.	Ms. Pat Jewell	(812) 948–9161
15	Area 15 Agency on Aging, Inc., Hoosier Uplands Economic Corp., 521 Main St., Mitchell, Ind. 47446.	Mr. David Miller	(812) 849–4457

IOWA

(Federal Region VII)

STATE AGENCY ON AGING

Betty Grandquist, Executive Director
DEPARTMENT OF ELDER AFFAIRS
Suite 236, Jewett Building
914 Grand Avenue
Des Moines, Iowa 50319
(515) 281-5187

AREA AGENCIES

PSA	Area agency address	Director and telephone number
1	Area 1 Area Agency on Aging, 808 River Street, Decorah, Iowa 52101.	Mr. Bruce Butters . . . .(319) 382-2941
2/5/12	Area Agency on Aging of North Central Iowa, 500 College Drive, Mason City, Iowa 50401.	Mr. Donald Ryerkerk . . . . .(515) 424-0678
3	Iowa Lakes Are Agency on Aging, 2 Grand Avenue, P.O. Box 3010, Spencer, Iowa 51301.	Mr. Greg Anlinker . . . .(712) 262-1775
4	Area 4 Agency on Aging; SIMPCO, 400 Orpheum Electric Bldg., Sioux City, Iowa 51102.	Mr. Rich Motz . . . .(712) 279-6286
6/7	Hawkeye Valley Area Agency, 620 Mulberry Street, P.O. Box 2576, Waterloo, Iowa 50704.	Ms. Donna Rhone . . . .(319) 233-5214
8	Scenic Valley Area Agency on Aging, 801 Davis Avenue, Dubuque, Iowa 52001.	Ms. Linda McDonald . . . . .(319) 588-3970

9	Great River Bend Bi-State Metropolitan Planning Comm., 1504 Third Avenue, Rock Island, Ill. 61201.	Mr. Marvin Webb	(309) 793–6334
10	Heritage Area Agency on Aging, Kirkwood Community College, 6301 Kirkwood Blvd. S.W., Cedar Rapids, Iowa 52406.	Mr. Russ Proffitt	(319) 398–5559
11	Crossroads of Iowa Area Agency on Aging, 1040 4th Street, Des Moines 50314.	Ms. Dorothy Tremel	(515) 244–4046
13	S.W. Eight Area XIII Area Agency on Aging, 3319 Nebraska Avenue, P.O. Box 368, Council Bluffs, Iowa 51502.	Mr. Frank Kowal	(712) 328–2540
14	Area XIV Agency on Aging, 228 North Pine, Creston, Iowa 50801.	Ms. Lois Houston	(515) 782–4040
15	SIEDA Area Agency on Aging, 226 W. Main St., P.O. Box 658, Ottumwa, Iowa 52501.	Ms. Peggy Amos	(515) 682-8741
16	Southwest Iowa Area Agency on Aging, 510 Jefferson Street, Burlington, Iowa 52601.	Ms. Phyllis White	(319) 752–5433

KANSAS

(Federal Region VII)

STATE AGENCY ON AGING

Esther Wolf, Acting Secretary
DEPARTMENT ON AGING
610 West Tenth
Topeka, Kansas 66612
(913) 296–4986

AREA AGENCIES

PSA	Area agency address	Director and telephone number
1	Wyandotte-Leavenworth County Area Agency on Aging, 9400 State Ave., Kansas City, Kans. 66112.	Mr. Art Collins .... (913) 788–7820
2	Central Plains Area Agency on Aging, 510 N. Main St., Wichita, Kans. 67603.	Ms. Irene Hart .... (316) 268–7298
3	Northwest Kansas Area Agency on Aging, 301 West 13th, Room 306, Hays, Kans. 67601.	Ms. Ellene Davis .... (913) 628–8204
4	Jayhawk Area Agency on Aging, 1195 Buchanan, No. 103, Topeka, Kans. 66604.	Ms. Donna Kidd .... (913) 235–1367
5	Southeast Kansas Area Agency on Aging, 1500 W. 7th St., Box 269, Chanute, Kans. 66720.	Mr. Jerry Williams .... (316) 431–2980
6	Southwest Kansas Area Agency on Aging, 108 North 14, P.O. Box 1636, Dodge City, Kans. 67801.	Mr. David Geist .... (316) 225–0510

7	Mid-America Council on Aging, 132 South Main, Ottawa, Kans. 66067.	Ms. Shirley Higdon	(913) 242–7200
8	North Central Flint Hills Area Agency on Aging, 2601 Anderson Ave., Manhattan, Kans. 66502.	Ms. Monda Spool	(913) 776–9294
9	Northeast Kansas Area Agency on Aging, 107 Oregon West, P.O. Box 456, Hiawatha, Kans. 66434.	Ms. Anna Mae Shaffer	(913) 742–7152
10	South Central Kansas Area Agency on Aging, P.O. Box 1122, Arkansas, Kans. 67005.	Ms. Betty Londeen	(316) 442-0268
11	Human Resources and Aging Department, 130 N. Cherry, Olathe, Kans. 66061.	Ms. Trish Kelley Moore	(913) 782-7188

KENTUCKY

(Federal Region IV)

STATE AGENCY ON AGING

Prudence Moore, Director
DIVISION FOR AGING SERVICES
Department of Human Resources
DHR Building – 6th Floor
275 East Main Street
Frankfort, Kentucky 40601
(502) 564–6930

AREA AGENCIES

PSA	Area agency address	Director and telephone number
1	Purchase Area Development District, U.S. Highway 45 N., P.O. Box 588, Mayfield, Ky. 42066.	Ms. Davida French ....(502) 247–7171
2	Pennyrile Area Development District, 300 Hammond Drive, Hopkinsville, Ky. 42240.	Ms. Agnes Davis ....(502) 886–9484
3	Green River Area Agency on Aging, 3860 U.S. Highway 60 West, Owensboro, Ky. 42301.	Ms. Nelda Barnett ....(502) 926–4433
4	Barren River Development District, 740 E. 10th St., P.O. Box 2120, Bowling Green, Ky. 42101.	Mr. Bill Cooper ....(502) 781-2381
5	Lincoln Trail Area Development District, 702 College St., Elizabethtown, Ky. 42701.	Ms. Becky McMakin-Smith. .(502) 769–2393

6	Kentuckiana Regional Planning and Development Agency, 912 East Broadway, Louisville, Ky. 40202.	Ms. Betty Rulander	(502) 589-4406
7	Northern Kentucky Area Development District, 7505 Sussex Dr., Suite 8, Florence, Ky. 41042.	Ms. Deanna Skees	(606) 283-1885
8	Buffalo Trace Area Development District, 327 West Second St., Maysville, Ky. 41056.	Ms. Jeanette Kropa	(606) 564-6894
9	Gateway Area Development District, Main & State Streets, P.O. Box 107, Owingsville, Ky. 40360.	Mr. Charles Jones	(606) 739-5191
10	FIVCO Area Agency on Aging, 3000 Louisa St., Box 636, Catlettsburg, Ky. 41129.	Ms. Brenda Ward	(606) 739-5191
11	Big Sandy Area Development District, Municipal Bldg., Lake Shore Dr., 2d floor, Prestonburg, Ky. 41653.	Ms. Phyllis Stanley	(606) 886-2374
12	Kentucky River Area Development District, 381 Perry Park Rd., Hazard, Ky. 41701.	Ms. Ruth Ann Miller	(606) 436-3158
13	Cumberland Valley Area Agency on Aging, CVADD Bldg., Route 13, London, Ky. 40741.	Mr. Phillip Martin	(606) 864-7391
14	Lake Cumberland Area Development District, P.O. Box 570, Russell Springs, Ky. 42642.	Mr. Jim Simpson	(502) 343-3154
15	Bluegrass Area Agency on Aging, 3220 Nicholasville Rd., Lexington, Ky. 50402.	Ms. Peggy Chadwick	(606) 272-6656

LOUISIANA

(Federal Region VI)

STATE AGENCY ON AGING

Sandra Adams, Director
OFFICE OF ELDERLY AFFAIRS
P.O. Box 80374
Baton Rouge, Louisiana 70898
(504) 925-1700

AREA AGENCIES

PSA	Area agency address	Director and telephone number
1	Allen Council on Aging, Drawer E-L, 600 East 7th Avenue, Oakdale, La. 71463.	Mr. Billy Ray Smith ....(318) 335-3195
2	Beauregard Council on Aging, P.O. Drawer 534, 112 Jefferson St., DeRidder, La. 71634.	Ms. Juanita LaBue ....(318) 463-6578
3	Bienville Council on Aging, Room 112 Courthouse, Arcadia, La. 71001.	Mr. Elton A. Lamkin ....(318) 263-8936
4	Bossier Council on Aging, P.O. Box 5606, 701 Coleman, Bossier City, La. 71111.	Ms. Vicki Brunson ....(318) 742-8993
5	Caddo Council on Aging, 4015 Greenwood Rd., Shreveport, La. 71109.	Ms. Myrtle Pickering ......(318) 636-7956
6	Calcasieu Council on Aging, P.O. Box 6403, Lake Charles, La. 70606.	Ms. Linda Woodel ....(318) 433-1627
7	Caldwell Council on Aging, P.O. Box 1498, Main Street, Columbia, La. 71418.	Ms. Marjorie Harris ....(318) 649-2584

8	Cameron Council on Aging, P.O. Box 421, D Street, Cameron, La. 70631.	Ms. Dinah Vaughan	(318) 775-5668
9	Clauborne Council on Aging, 608 East 4th St., Homer, La. 71040.	Ms. Gail Robillard	(318) 927-6922
10	Desoto Council on Aging, P.O. Box 1003, 519 Franklin St., Mansfield, La. 71052.	Ms. Dwena Henry	(318) 872-2691
11	East Baton Rouge Council on Aging, 2905 Fairfields Avenue, Baton Rouge, La. 70802.	Ms. Sharon LaFleur	(504) 389-4916
12	Jefferson Council on Aging, P.O. Box 6878, 4425 Utica St., Metairie, La. 70006.	Mr. Thomas Laughlin	(504) 888-5880
13	LaFourche Council on Aging, 710 Church St., P.O. Box 187, Lockport, La. 70374.	Ms. Sandra Barrios	(504) 532-2381
14	Lincoln Council on Aging, 109 South Sparta, Ruston, La. 71270.	Ms. Sharon Slaughter	(318) 255-5070
15	Madison Council on Aging, 211 S. Chestnut St., P.O. Drawer 352, Tallulah, La. 71282.	Mr. Audrey S. Ogden	(318) 574-4101
16	Morehouse Council on Aging, P.O. Box 1471, Elm Street, Bastrop, La. 71221-1471.	Mr. Reggie Defreese	(318) 281-6127
17	Natchitoches Council on Aging, P.O. Box 566, 220 East 5th Street, Natchitoches, La. 71457-0566.	Ms. Norma Metoyer	(318) 352-8490
18	New Orleans Council on Aging, P.O. Box 19067, 2400 Canal Street, New Orleans, La. 70179-0067.	Mr. George Gates	(504) 821-4121
19	Ouchita Council on Aging, 1209 Oliver Rd., Monroe, La. 71207-4363.	Mr. Joseph Nastasi	(318) 387-0535
20	Plaquemines Council on Aging, P.O. Box 992, Highway 23, Port Sulphur, La. 70083.	Ms. Carolyn Turlich	(504) 564-3220
21	Red River Council on Aging, P.O. Box 688, 1825 Front Street, Coushatta, La. 71019.	Ms. Mary Wailes	(318) 932-5419
22	Sabine Council on Aging, 750 Railroad Avenue, Many, La. 71449.	Mr. W. Glen Starks	(318) 256-5278
23	St. Bernard Council on Aging, 1818 Center Street, Arabi, La. 70032.	Ms. Alfreda Earhart	(504) 279-0444
24	St. Charles Council on Aging, 117 Angus Drive, Luling, La. 70070.	Ms. Margaret Powe	(504) 785-9574

LOUISIANA—Continued

PSA	Area agency address	Director and telephone number
25	St. James Area Agency on Aging, P.O. Box 87, St. James Parish Courthouse, Department of Human Services, Convent, La. 70723.	Mr. Charles Winchester . . . . .(504) 562–2300
26	St. John Council on Aging, P.O. Drawer H, 805 W. Airline Highway, Laplace, La. 70068.	Ms. Barbara Gralapp . . . . . .(504) 652–3660
27	St. Tammany Council on Aging, 328 East Boston, P.O. Box 171, Covington, La. 70433.	Ms. Gloria Sellers . . . .(504) 892–0377
28	Tensas Council on Aging, 104 Panola, P.O. Box 726, St. Joseph, La. 71366.	Ms. Dorothy Morgan . . . . . .(318) 766–3770
29	Terrebonne Council on Aging, P.O. Box 10066, Station 1, Houma, La. 70360.	Ms. Carol L. Matherne . . . . .(504) 868–7701
30	Webster Council on Aging, P.O. Box 913, 316 McIntyre, Minden, La. 71055.	Ms. Dathene Brown . . . .(318) 377–0141
31	West Carroll Council on Aging, 207 East Jefferson, P.O. Box 1058, Oak Grove, La. 71263.	Ms. Faye Long . . . .(318) 428–4217
32	Capital Area Agency on Aging, P.O. Box 66638, 213 SE Acadian Thruway, Baton Rouge, La 70896.	Mr. Brad Smith . . . .(504) 343–9278
33	Kisatchie Delta Regional Planning and Development District, P.O. Box 12248, Alexandria, La. 71315–2248.	Ms. Kristin Duke . . . .(318) 487–5454
34	Cajun Area Agency on Aging, 1304 Bertrand Dr., Suite F–6, Lafayette, La. 70506.	Dr. Alex Romano . . . .(318) 237–7744
35	North Delta Planning and Development District, 2115 Justice St., Monroe, La. 71201.	Ms. LaNell Winston . . . .(318) 387–2572

MAINE

(Federal Region I)

STATE AGENCY ON AGING

Christine Gianopoulos, Acting Director
BUREAU OF MAINE'S ELDERLY
Department of Human Services
State House – Station #11
Augusta, Maine 04333
(207) 289-2561

AREA AGENCIES

PSA	Area agency address	Director and telephone number
1	Aroostock Area Agency on Aging, 33 Davis Street, P.O. Box 1288, Presque Isle, Maine 04769.	Mr. Stephen Farnham ......(207) 764-3396
2	Eastern Area Agency on Aging, Twin City Shopping Plaza, P.O. Box 70, Brewer, Maine 04412.	Ms. Madeleine Freeman ....(207) 941-2865
3	Central Maine Area Agency on Aging, Alkin Building, AMHI, P.O. Box 510, Augusta, Maine 04330.	Ms. Muriel Scott ....(207) 622-9344
4	West Area Agency on Aging, 465 Main St., P.O. Box 659, Lewiston, Maine 04240.	Ms. Eloise Moreau ....(207) 784-8797
5	Southern Maine Area Agency on Aging Inc., 237 Oxford St., P.O. Box 10480, Portland, Maine 04104.	Mr. Laurence Gross ....(207) 775-6503

MARYLAND

(Federal Region III)

STATE AGENCY ON AGING

Rosalie Abrams, Director
OFFICE ON AGING
State Office Building
301 West Preston Street, Rm. #1004
Baltimore, Maryland 21201
(301) 225-1100

AREA AGENCIES

PSA	Area agency address	Director and telephone number
1	Garrett County Area Agency on Aging, 360 W. Liberty St., P.O. Box 449, Oakland, Md. 21550.	Ms. Margo Van Diver ......(301) 334-9431
2	Allegany County Area Agency on Aging, 19 Federick St., Cumberland, Md. 21502.	Ms. Mary Sue Cerutti ......(301) 777-5970
3	Washington County Area Agency on Aging, 9 Public Sq., Alexander House, Hagerstown, Md. 21740.	Mr. Ralph Garver ....(301) 790-0275
4	Frederick County Commission on Aging, 600 N. Bentz St., Bldg. 7, Basement, Frederick, Md. 21701.	Ms. Patricia Throne ....(301) 694-1604
5	Carroll County Office on Aging, West End School, Schoolhouse Ave., Westminster, Md. 21157.	Ms. Jolene Sullivan ....(301) 875-3342
6	Baltimore County Department of Aging, 611 Central Ave., Towson, Md. 21204.	Mr. J. Timothy Fagan ......(301) 494-2107

7	Baltimore City Area Agency on Aging, 1114 Cathedral St., Baltimore, Md. 21201.	Ms. Mary Jane Lyman	(301) 396-5780
8	Harford County Area Agency on Aging, Equitable Bldg., 145 North Hickory Avenue, Bel Air, Md. 21014.	Mr. James Macgill	(301) 879-2000
9	Area Agency on Aging, 250 Hungerford Dr., Rockville, Md. 20850.	Mr. Donald Wassmann	(301) 279-1920
10	Howard County Office on Aging, John Carroll Bldg., 1st floor, 3450 Courthouse Dr., Ellicott City, Md. 21043.	Ms. Vivian Reid	(301) 992-2327
11	Anne Arundel County Area Agency on Aging, Anne Arundel Center North, 101 N. Crain Highway, Glen Burnie, Md. 21061.	Ms. Janet Owens	(301) 787-6707
12	Prince Georges' County Area Agency on Aging, County Services Bldg., 5012 Rhode Island Ave., Hyattsville, Md. 20781.	Ms. Sue Ward	(301) 699-2797
13	Calvert County Office on Aging, 450 West Dares Beach Rd., P.O. Box 221, Prince Frederick, Md. 20678.	Ms. Bettina Dubas	(301) 535-4606
14	Charles County Aging Services, P.O. Box B, (Courthouse) No. 5 Oak Ave., La Plata, Md. 20646.	Ms. Margaret Cheseldine	(301) 934-3776
15	St. Marys County Office on Aging, 245 N. Washington St., Governmental Center, P.O. Box 653, Leonardtown, Md. 20650.	Ms. Billye McGaharn	(301) 475-5621
16	Upper Shore Aging, Inc., 400 High St., 2d floor, Chestertown, Md. 21620.	Ms. Pat Clarke	(301) 778-6000
17	Queen Anne's County Office on Aging, County Annex Bldg., P.O. Box 20, 412 N. Commerce St., Centreville, Md. 21617.	Mr. Irving Pinder	(301) 758-0848
18	MAC, Inc. Area Agency on Aging, 1504 Riverside Dr., Salisbury, Md. 21801.	Ms. Margaret Bradford	(301) 742-0505

MASSACHUSETTS

(Federal Region I)

STATE AGENCY ON AGING

Paul J. Lanzikos, Secretary
EXECUTIVE OFFICE OF ELDER AFFAIRS
38 Chauncy Street
Boston, Massachusetts 02111
(617) 727-7750

AREA AGENCIES

PSA	Area agency address	Director and telephone number
1A	Elder Services of Berkshire County, Inc., 100 North St., Pittsfield, Mass. 01201.	Mr. Frederick Whitham . . . . .(413) 499-1353
1B	Franklin County Home Care Corp., Central St., Turners Falls, Mass. 01376.	Ms. Janice L. Gibeau . . . .(413) 863-9565
1C	Highland Valley Elder Services Center, Inc., 320 Riverside Drive, Northampton, Mass. 01060.	Mr. Robert Gallant . . . .(413) 586-2000
1D	Holyoke/Chicopee Home Care, 198 High St., Holyoke, Mass. 01040.	Ms. Priscilla Chalmers . . . . .(413) 538-9020
1E	Greater Springfield Senior Services, Inc., 66 Industry Ave., Springfield, Mass. 01104.	Ms. Patricia Clark . . . .(413) 781-8800
2	Region II Area Agency on Aging, 1128 Main St., Holden, Mass. 01520.	Mr. Bernard O'Neill . . . .(617) 829-5364
3A	Senior Home Care Services, 2 Main St., Gloucester, Mass. 01930.	Mr. Guntis Licis . . . .(617) 281-1750

3B	North Shore Elder Services, Inc., 484 Lowell St., Peabody, Mass. 01960.	Ms. Janet McAveney	(617) 535-6220
3C	Greater Lynn Senior Services, Inc., 8 Silsbee Street, Lynn, Mass. 01902.	Mr. Vincent Lique	(617) 599-0110
3D	Chalsea/Revere/Winthrop Home Care Center, Inc., 300 Broadway, P.O. Box 189, Revere, Mass. 02151.	Mr. James Cunningham	(617) 286-0550
3E	Mystic Valley Elder Home Care, Inc., 661 Main St., suite 110, Malden, Mass. 02148.	Mr. Daniel O'Leary	(617) 324-7705
3F	Somerville/Cambridge Home Care Corp., 1 Davis Sq., 2d floor, Somerville, Mass. 02144.	Mr. John F. O'Neill, Jr.,	(617) 628-2601
3G	Minuteman Home Care Corp., 83 Hartwell Ave., Lexington, Mass. 02173.	Ms. Joan Butler-West	(617) 862-6200
3H	West Suburban Elder Services, Inc., 124 Watertown St., Parker Office Bldg., Watertown, Mass. 02173.	Ms. Nancy Dale	(617) 926-4100
3J	Baypath Senior Citizens Services, Inc., P.O. Box 2625, Building #13, Cushing Hospital, Framingham, Mass. 01701.	Mr. Don Medd	(617) 620-0840
3K	Health and Social Services Consortium, Inc., IGO Bldg., Carpenter St., Foxboro, Mass. 02035.	Ms. Jean Carbone	(617) 543-2611
3L	South Shore Home Care Services, Inc., 639 Granite St., P.O. Box 367, Braintree, Mass. 02184.	Ms. Susan Young	(617) 848-3910
4A	Old Colony Elderly Services, Inc., 231 West Main St., P.O. Box 1586, Brockton, Mass. 02043.	Mr. William Goyette	(617) 584-1561
4B	Bristol Elder Services, Inc., 182 N. Main St., Fall River, Mass. 02720.	Ms. Carol A. Nagle	(617) 675-2101
4C	Coast Line Elder Services, Inc., 106 Huttleston Avenue, Fairhaven, Mass. 02719.	Mr. Charles Sisson	(617) 999-6400
4D	Elder Services of Cape Cod & Islands, Inc., 68 Route 134, South Dennis, Mass. 02660.	Ms. Sally Fogarty	(617) 394-4630
5	Elder Services of the Merrimack Valley, 420 Common St., Lawrence, Mass. 01840.	Ms. Roseanne DiStefano	(617) 683-7747
6	Boston Commission on Affairs of the Elderly, 1 City Hall Sq., room 271, Boston, Mass. 02201.	Mr. Michael Taylor	(617) 725-4366

MICHIGAN

(Federal Region V)

STATE AGENCY ON AGING

Olivia Maynard, Director
OFFICE OF SERVICES TO THE AGING
P.O. Box 30026
Lansing, Michigan 48909
(517) 373-8230

AREA AGENCIES

PSA	Area agency address	Director and telephone number
1A	Detroit Area Agency on Aging, 3110 Book Bldg., 1249 Washington Blvd., Detroit, Mich. 48226.	Mr. Paul Bridgewater ......(313) 222-5330
1B	Region I-B Area Agency on Aging, 29508 Southfield Rd., suite 100, Southfield, Mich. 48076.	Ms. Sandra K. Reminga ....(313) 569-0333
1C	The Senior Alliance, 3850 2nd St., suite 160, Wayne, Mich. 48184.	Ms. Donelda Thompson ....(313) 722-2830
2	Region II Commission on Aging, 3221 North Adrian Dr., P.O. Box 649, Adrian, Mich. 49221-0646.	Mr. Charles L. Anson ......(517) 265-7881
3	Southcentral Michigan Commission on Aging, 8135 Cox's Dr., suite 1-C, Portage, Mich. 49002.	Ms. Mary Sawicki ....(616) 343-4996
4	Region IV Area Agency on Aging, 2919 Division Street, St. Joseph, Mich. 49085.	Mr. Robert L. Dolsen ....(616) 983-0177
5	Valley Area Agency on Aging, 708 Root St., room 110, Flint, Mich. 48503.	Ms. Valeria Conerly ....(313) 239-7671

6	Tri-County Office on Aging, 500 West Washtenaw, Lansing, Mich. 48933.	Ms. Roxanna Peterson	(517) 483-4150
7	Region VII Area Agency on Aging, 1200 North Madison Ave., East Community Center, Bay City, Mich. 48706-5955.	Mr. Mohammed Y. Khan	(517) 893-4506
8	Area Agency on Aging of Western Michigan, Inc., 540 Two Fountain Place, Grand Rapids, Mich. 49503.	Mr. Lawrence L. Murray, Jr.	(616) 456-5664
9	Northeast Michigan Community Services, 2373 Gordon Rd., P.O. Box 1038, Alpena, Mich. 49707.	Ms. Sue Schuler	(517) 356-3474
10	Northwest Michigan Area Agency on Aging, 1609 Park Drive, P.O. Box 2010, Traverse City, Mich. 49685.	Mr. Ronald Crummel	(616) 947-8920
11	Region XI Area Agency on Aging, UPCAP Services, Inc., 118 North 22nd St., Escanaba, Mich. 49829.	Mr. Robert E. Olsen	(906)786-4701
14	Region XIV Area Planning Council on Aging, 315 West Webster, Muskegon, Mich. 49440.	Ms. Rosanne Richards	(616) 722-7811

MINNESOTA

(Federal Region V)

STATE AGENCY ON AGING

Gerald Bloedow, Executive Director
BOARD ON AGING
Metro Square Building – Room 204
Seventh and Robert Streets
St. Paul, Minnesota 55101
(612) 296–2544

AREA AGENCIES

PSA	Area agency address	Director and telephone number
1	Northwest Regional Development Commission, P.O. Box E, Brooks Ave., South, The River, Falls, Minn. 56701.	Ms. Faith Rud . . . .(218) 281–1396
2	Region II Area Agency on Aging, Headwater Regional Development Commission, 722 15th St., Box 906, Bemidji, Minn. 56601.	Mr. Alan Goldberg . . . .(218) 751–3108
3	Arrowhead Area Agency on Aging, 330 Canal Park Drive, Duluth, Minn. 55802.	Ms. Joyce Bohn Allen . . . . . .(218) 722–5545
4	West Central Area Agency on Aging, P.O. Box 726, 112 West Washington Ave., Fergus Falls, Minn. 56536.	Ms. Laurel Sorlie . . . .(218) 739–4617
5	Region V Area Agency on Aging, Region V Regional Development Commission, 611 Iowa Ave., Staples, Minn. 56479.	Ms. Barbara Card . . . .(218) 894–3233
6E	Mid-Minnesota Regional Development Commission, 333 West 6th St., Willmar, Minn. 56201.	Mr. Robert Otto . . . .(612) 235–8504

6W	Region VI, West Area Agency on Aging, Upper Minn. Valley Regional Development Commission, 323 West Schlieman, Appleton, Minn. 56208.	Mr. Paul Michaelson	(612) 289-1981
7E	Region VII Area Agency on Aging, 110 South Park, St. Mora, Minn. 55051.	Mr. Roger Ames	(612) 679-4065
7W	Central Minnesota Council on Aging, Corporate Center, 26 N. 6th Ave., St. Cloud, Minn. 56301.	Ms. Donna Walberg	(612) 253-9349
8	Southwest Regional Development Commission's Aging Program, 2524 Broadway, Box 265, Slayton, Minn. 56172.	Ms. Maddy Forsberg	(507) 836-8549
9	Region Nine Area Agency on Aging, 410 South 5th St., Box 3367, Mankato, Minn. 56001.	Ms. Carol Bishop	(507) 387-5643
10	Southeastern Minn. Area Agency on Aging, 121 North Broadway, room 302, Rochester, Minn. 55904.	Ms. Connie Bagley	(507) 288-6944
11	Twin Cities Area Agency, Metropolitan Council, 300 Metro Square, 7th and Robert, St. Paul, Minn. 55101.	Ms. LaRhae Knatterud	(612) 291-6497
12	Minnesota Chippewa Tribe, Area Agency on Aging, P.O. Box 217, Cass Lake, Minn. 56633.	Ms. Luella Seelye	(218) 335-2252

MISSISSIPPI

(Federal Region IV)

STATE AGENCY ON AGING

David K. Brown, Director
COUNCIL ON AGING
301 West Pearl Street
Jackson, Mississippi 39203–3092
(601) 949–2070

AREA AGENCIES

PSA	Area agency address	Director and telephone number
1	North Delta Area Agency on Aging, P.O. Box 1244, 130 Lefleur Ave., Clarksdale, Miss. 38614.	Ms. Gloria Dear . . . .(601) 627–3401
2	South Delta Area Agency on Aging, P.O. Box 1776, 124 South Broadway, Greenville, Miss. 38702.	Ms. Sylvia Jackson . . . .(601) 378–3831
3	North Central Planning and Development District, Aging Division, P.O. Box 668, Highway 51 South, Winona, Miss. 38967.	Mr. Carl Cooper . . . .(601) 283–2675
4	Golden Triangle Planning and Development District, Aging Division, P.O. Drawer DN, Memorial Hall, Room 215, Mississippi State, Miss. 39762.	Mr. Bobby Gann . . . .(601) 325–3855
5	Three Rivers Planning and Development District, Aging Division, 75 South Main, P.O. Drawer B Pontotoc, Miss. 38863.	Ms. Jane Mapp . . . .(601) 489–2415

6	North East Planning and Development District, Aging Division, Highway 4 N. 30 Bypass, P.O. Box 600, Booneville, Miss. 38829.	Mr. R.C. Anderson	(601) 728-6248
7	Central Mississippi Area Agency on Aging, 2675 River Ridge Rd., P.O. Box 4935, Jackson, Miss. 39216.	Ms. Betty Burgess	(601) 981-1511
8	East Central Planning and Development District, 410 Decatur St., P.O. Box 499, Newton, Miss. 39345.	Ms. Myrtle Burton	(601) 683-2007
9	Southern Mississippi Area Agency on Aging, 1020 32d Ave., Gulfport, Miss. 39501.	Ms. Jane Kennedy	(601) 868-2311 1-(800) 222-9504
10	Southwest Mississippi Area Agency on Aging, P.O. Box 429, Meadville, Miss. 39653.	Mr. Johnny Smith	(601) 384-5881

MONTANA

(Federal Region VIII)

STATE AGENCY ON AGING

Norma Harris, Administrator
COMMUNITY SERVICES DIVISION
P.O. Box 4210
Helena, Montana 59604
(406) 444-3865

AREA AGENCIES

PSA	Area agency address	Director and telephone number
1	Area Agency on Aging, 123 North Merrill, Glendive, Mont. 59330.	Ms. Lori Brengle ....(406) 365-3364
2	Area Agency on Aging, 236 Main St., Roundup, Mont. 59072	Ms. Karen Erdie ....(406) 323-1320
3	North Central Area Agency on Aging, 323 South Main St., Conrad, Mont. 59425.	Ms. Beverly Robinson ......(406) 278-5662
4	Rocky Mountain Development Council, Area Agency on Aging, 201 South Main, P.O. Box 721, Helena, Mont. 59601.	Mr. Roger Ala ....(406) 442-1552
5	Area Agency on Aging, 115 East Pennsylvania Ave., Anaconda, Mont. 59711.	Ms. Jane Anderson ....(406) 563-3110
6	Western Montana Area Agency on Aging, Box 4027, Polson, Mont. 59860.	Mr. Duane Lutke ....(406) 833-6211
7	Tribal Elders Program, Area Agency on Aging, 2303 Grand Ave., suite 10, Billings, Mont. 59102.	Mr. Steve Williamson ......(406) 652-3113

8	Cascade County Council on Aging, 1601 2d Ave. North, Great Falls, Mont. 59401.	Ms. Nancy Wilson	(406) 761-1919
9	Flathead County Council on Aging, Area 9, 723 5th Ave. East, Kalispell, Mont. 59901.		(406) 752-5300
10	Hill County Council on Aging, 2 West 2d St., Havre, Mont. 59501.	Ms. Evelyn Havskjold	(406) 265-5464
11	Missoula County Council on Aging, 900 North Orange, suite 106, Missoula, Mont. 59802.	Ms. Pearl Bruno	(406) 728-7682

NEBRASKA

(Federal Region VII)

STATE AGENCY ON AGING

Betsy Palmer, Director
DEPARTMENT ON AGING
P.O. Box 95044
301 Centennial Mall–South
Lincoln, Nebraska 68509
(402) 471–2306

AREA AGENCIES

PSA	Area agency address	Director and telephone number
A	Eastern Nebraska Office on Aging, 885 South 72d St., Omaha, Nebr. 68114.	Ms. Beverly Griffith . . . . . . (402) 444–6536
B	Lincoln Area Agency on Aging, 129 North 10th St., room 241, Lincoln, Nebr. 68508.	Mr. James Zietlow . . . . (402) 471–7022
C	Northeast Nebraska Area Agency on Aging, North Stone Bldg., Regional Center Grounds, P.O. Box 1447, Norfolk, Nebr. 68701.	. . . . (402) 371–7454
F	South Central Nebraska Area Agency on Aging, 124 West 46th St., Kearney, Nebr. 68847.	Mr. Dennis Loose . . . . (308) 234–1851
G	Midland Area Agency on Aging, 500 North Denver, P.O. Box 905, Hastings, Nebr. 68901.	Mr. Jerry Ryan . . . . (402) 463–4565

H	Blue Rivers Area Agency on Aging, Gage County Courthouse, room 24, Beatrice, Nebr. 68310.	Mr. Fred Holtz	(402) 223-3124
J	West Central Nebraska Area Agency on Aging, 200 South Silber Ave., North Platte, Nebr. 69101.	Mr. Bob Fosbinder	(308) 534-6780
L	Aging Office of Western Nebraska, 4502 Ave. I, Scottsbluff, Nebr. 69361.	Mr. Victor Walker	(308) 635-0851

NEVADA*

(Federal Region IX)

STATE AGENCY ON AGING

Myla Florence, Executive Director
DIVISION ON AGING
Department of Human Resources
505 East King Street
Kinkead Building - Room 101
Carson City, Nevada 89710
(702) 885-4210

*The State of Nevada serves as a single planning and service area.

NEW HAMPSHIRE*

(Federal Region I)

STATE AGENCY ON AGING

Richard Chevrefils, Director
COUNCIL ON AGING
105 Loudon Road – Bldg. #3
Concord, New Hampshire 03301
(603) 271–2751

*The State of New Hampshire serves as a single planning and service area.

NEW JERSEY

(Federal Region II)

STATE AGENCY ON AGING

Ann Zahora, Director
DIVISION ON AGING
Department of Community Affairs
P.O. Box 2768
363 West State Street
Trenton, New Jersey 08625
(609) 292–4833

AREA AGENCY

PSA	Area agency address	Director and telephone number
1	Atlantic County Division on Aging, 1625 Atlantic Ave., 2nd floor, Atlantic City, N.J. 08401.	Mr. Gerald DelRosso . . . .(609) 345–6700
2	Bergen County Office on Aging, 355 Main St., Hackensack, N.J. 07601–5875.	Mr. Joseph Rutch . . . .(201) 646–2625
3	Burlington County Office on Aging, 49 Rancocas Rd., Mount Holly, N.J. 08060.	Ms. Lindy Coffey . . . .(609) 265–5000
4	Camden County Office on Aging, 120 White Horse Pike, Suite 103, Haddon Heights, N.J. 08035.	Mr. Edward Donahue . . . . . .(609) 546–6404
5	Cape May County Office on Aging, P.O. Box 222, Social Services Bldg., Rio Grande, N.J. 08242.	Mr. William Sheva . . . .(609) 886–2784

NEW JERSEY—Continued

PSA	Area agency address	Director and telephone number
6	Cumberland County Office on Aging, Administration Bldg., 790 East Commerce St., Bridgeton, N.J. 08302.	Mr. Henry Ricci . . . .(609) 451-8000
7	Essex County Office on Aging, 15 South Munn Avenue, East Orange, N.J. 07018.	Mr. Larry Coumo . . . .(201) 678-9700
8	Gloucester County Department on Aging, 44 Delaware St., Woodbury, N.J. 08096.	Ms. Margaret Mendoza . . . . .(609) 853-3312
9	Hudson County Office on Aging, 114 Clifton Pl., Murdoch Hall, Jersey City, N.J. 07304.	Mr. William A. Macchi . . . . .(201) 434-6900
10	Hunterdon County Office on Aging, 6 Gauntt Place, Flemington, N.J. 08822.	Ms. Rosemarie Doremus . . . .(201) 788-1362
11	Mercer County Office on Aging, Mercer County Administration Bldg., 640 S. Broad St., P.O. Box 8068, Trenton, N.J. 08650.	Mr. Carl F. West . . . .(609) 989-6661
12	Middlesex County Office on Aging, 841 Georges Rd., North Brunswick, N.J. 08902.	Mr. George Coakley . . . .(201) 745-3293
13	Monmouth County Office on Aging, Hall of Records Annex, E. Main St., Freehold, N.J. 07728.	Sr. Mary Simon . . . .(201) 431-7450
14	Morris County Office on Aging, Court House, CN 900, Morristown, N.J. 07960.	Mr. Norman VanHouten . . . .(201) 829-8539
15	Ocean County Office on Aging, CN-2191, Toms River, N.J. 08754.	Mr. Philip Rubenstein . . . . . .(201) 244-2121
16	Passaic County Office on Aging, 675 Goffle Rd., Hawthorne, N.J. 07506.	Ms. Bettie Barnes Anderson .(201) 881-4950
17	Salem County Office on Aging, Lakeview Complex, P.O. Box 276, Woodstown, N.J. 08098.	Ms. Constance G. Undy . . . .(609) 769-4150
18	Somerset County Office on Aging, Box 3000, Somerville, N.J. 08876.	Ms. Ruth Reader . . . .(201) 231-7175
19	Sussex County Office on Aging, 175 High St., Newton, N.J. 07860.	Mr. Robert Callahan . . . .(201) 383-5098

20	Union County Division on Aging, County Administration Bldg., 4th floor, Elizabethtown Plaza, Elizabeth, N.J. 07207.	Mr. Philip Pearlman ....(201) 527-4866
21	Warren County Office on Aging, Wayne Dumont Jr. Administration Bldg., Belvidere, N.J. 07823.	Ms. Annie B. Schneider .....(201) 475-8000

NEW MEXICO

(Federal Region VI)

STATE AGENCY ON AGING

Stephanie FallCreek, Executive Director
STATE AGENCY ON AGING
224 East Palace Ave., 4th floor
La Villa Rivera Building
Santa Fe, New Mexico 87501
(505) 827-7640

AREA AGENCIES

PSA	Area agency address	Director and telephone number
1	City of Albuquerque Administrator, P.O. Box 1293, Albuquerque, N. Mex. 87103.	Mr. Ken Villani ....(505) 766-7550
2	District II Area Agency on Aging, Inc., P.O. Box 2514, Santa Fe, N. Mex. 87501.	Mr. Norman Martinez ......(505) 983-3621
3	Eastern New Mexico Area Agency on Aging, Inc., 901 West 13th Street, P.O. Box 2083, Clovis, N. Mex. 88101.	Mr. Fred Gisler ....(505) 769-1613
4	Southwestern New Mexico Area Agency on Aging, Inc.,Mesilla Community Center, P.O. Box 822, Mesilla, N. Mex. 88046.	Mr. Don Fahrenkroc ......(505) 525-0352

NEW YORK

(Federal Region II)

STATE AGENCY ON AGING

Eugene Callender, Director
Office for the Aging
New York State Executive Department
Empire State Plaza, Agency Building No. 2
Albany, NY 12223

AREA AGENCIES

PSA	Area agency address	Director and telephone number
1	Albany County Department for Aging & Handicapped, 112 State St., room 710, Albany, N.Y. 12207.	Mr. Richard Healy . . . .(518) 447-7180
2	Allegany County Office for Aging, 17 Court St., Belmont, N.Y. 14813.	Ms. Elizabeth E. Wattenberg (716) 268-9390
3	Broome County Office for the Aging, County Office Bldg., Government Plaza, Binghamton, N.Y. 13902.	Mr. Neal Lane . . . .(607) 772-2411
4	Cattaraugus County for the Aging, 255 N. Union St., Olean, N.Y. 14760.	Ms. Kathleen Horner . . . . . .(716) 375-4114
5	Cayuga County Office for Aging, 160 Genesee St., County Office Bldg., Auburn, N.Y. 13021.	Ms. Joan Gallo . . . .(315) 253-1226
6	Chautauqua County Office for the Aging, Hall R. Clothier Bldg., Mayville, N.Y. 14757.	Ms. Sandra L. Cliver . . . .(716) 753-4417

7	Chemung County Office for the Aging, 425–447 Pennsylvania Ave., Elmira, N.Y. 14904.	Mrs. Janice M. Ingersoll	(607) 737–5520
8	Chenango County Area Agency on Aging, County Office Bldg., 5 Court St., Norwich, N.Y. 13815.	Mrs. Denise Newvine	(607) 335–4624
9	Clinton County Office for the Aging, 137 Margaret St., Plattsburgh, N.Y. 12901.	Ms. Kathleen Laramie	(518) 565–4620
10	Columbia County Office on Aging, 71 North 3rd St., Hudson, N.Y. 12534.	Ms. Kit Carter	(518) 828–4258
11	Cortland County Office for the Aging, County Office Bldg., 60 Central Ave., P.O. Box 1172, Cortland, N.Y. 13045.	Ms. Nancy Hansen	(607) 753–5060
12	Delaware County Office for the Aging, 6 Court St., Delhi, N.Y. 13753.	Mr. Tom Briggs	(607) 746–6333
13	Dutchess County Office for the Aging, 488 Main St., Poughkeepsie, N.Y. 12601.	Mr. Hugh Miller	(914) 431–2465
14	Erie County Department of Senior Services, 95 Franklin St., Buffalo, N.Y. 14202.	Mr. Clifford Whitman	(716) 846–6046
15	Essex County Office for the Aging, Elizabethtown, N.Y. 12932.	Ms. Frances Filshie	(518) 873–6301
16	Franklin County Office for the Aging, County Court House, 89 West Main St., Malone, N.Y. 12953.	Ms. Janice Henderson	(518) 483–6767
17	Fulton County Office for the Aging, 1 E. Montgomery St., Johnstown, N.Y. 12095.	Ms. Kathryn Leitch	(518) 762–0650
18	Genesee County Office for the Aging, Batavia Genesee Senior Center, 2 Bank St., Batavia, N.Y. 14020.	Mr. William Lang	(716) 343–1611
19	Greene County Department for the Aging, 19 S. Jefferson Ave., P.O. Box 392, Catskill, N.Y. 12414.	Mr. Philip Schlenker	(518) 943–5332
21	Herkimer County Office for the Aging, County Office Bldg., Mary St., Herkimer, N.Y. 13350.	Mrs. Sylvia Bulson	(315) 867–1121
22	Jefferson County Office for the Aging, 1240 Coffeen St., Watertown, N.Y. 13601.	Mr. Douglas C. Gleason	(315) 782–9100
23	Lewis County Office for the Aging, Lewis County Ofc. Bldg., P.O. Box 408, Lowville, N.Y. 13367.	Mr. Randy Streeter	(315) 376–5313

NEW YORK—Continued

PSA	Area agency address	Director and telephone number
24	Livingston County Office for the Aging, Livingston County Campus, Bldg., 1, Mount Morris, N.Y. 14510.	Ms. Gloria Harrington .....(716) 658-2881
25	Madison County Office for the Aging, 43 E. Main St., Box 250, Rt. 20, Morrisville, N.Y. 13408.	Ms. Margaret Williams .....(315) 684-9424
26	Monroe County Office for the Aging, 375 Westfall Rd., Rochester, N.Y. 14620.	Mr. Gary R. Merritt ....(716) 442-6350
27	Montgomery Countywide Office for the Aging, 21 New St., Amsterdam, N.Y. 12010.	Ms. Janice Osowicki ....(518) 843-2300
28	Nassau County Department of Senior Citizens Affairs, 222 Willis Ave., Mineola, N.Y. 11501.	Ms. Adelaide Attard ....(516) 535-5990
29	Niagara County Office for the Aging, Switzer Bldg., 100 Davidson Rd., Lockport, N.Y. 14094.	Mr. Victor Cooke ....(716) 439-6044
30	Oneida County Office for the Aging, County Office Bldg., 800 Park Ave., Utica, N.Y. 13501.	Mrs. Vicki J. Wygant ......(315) 798-5771
31	Metropolitan Commission on Aging, 421 Montgomery St., Civic Center, 13th floor, Syracuse, N.Y. 13202.	Ms. Roslyn Bilford ....(315) 425-2362
32	Ontario County Office for the Aging, 120 North Main St., Canandaigua, N.Y. 14424.	Ms. Rita Canavan ....(716) 396-4040
33	Orange County Office for the Aging, 60 Erie St., 3d floor, Goshen, N.Y. 10924.	Mr. Joseph M. Dwyer ......(914) 294-5151
34	Orleans County Office for the Aging, Orleans County Admin. Bldg., 14016 Route 31, Albion, N.Y. 14411.	Ms. Carole Blake ....(716) 589-5673
35	Oswego County Office for the Aging, County Office Complex, 70 Bunner St., P.O. Box 3080, Oswego, N.Y. 13126.	Mrs. Mary King ....(315) 349-3484
36	Otsego County Office for the Aging, County Office Bldg., Cooperstown, N.Y. 13326.	Mr. Ed Bommer ....(607) 547-4233

37	Putnam County Office for Aging, 110 Old Route 6, Bldg. A, Carmel, N.Y. 10512.	Mr. William Huestis	(914) 225-1034
38	Rensselaer County Department for the Aging, 1700 7th Ave., Troy, N.Y. 12180.	Ms. Susan Baird	(518) 270-2730
39	Rockland County Office for the Aging, Health and Social Services Complex, Building B, Pomona, N.Y. 10970.	Ms. Virginia Weil	(914) 354-0200
40	St. Lawrence County Office for the Aging, County Office Bldg., Canton, N.Y. 13617.	Mr. Joseph Sears	(315) 379-2204
41	Saratoga County Office for the Aging, South Street School, Court St., Ballston Spa, N.Y. 12020.	Mr. Franklin C. DeMarinis	(518) 885-2212
42	Schenectady County Office for the Aging, 117 Nott Terr., Schenectady, N.Y. 12308.	Ms. Marilyn Haliski	(518) 382-8481
43	Schoharie County Office for the Aging, 122 E. Main St., Cobleskill, N.Y. 12043.	Mrs. Ethel Benninger	(518) 234-4219
44	Schuyler County Office for the Aging, 336-338 West Main St., Montour Falls, N.Y. 14865.	Mr. Richard Cole	(607) 535-7108
45	Seneca County Office for the Aging, P.O. Box 480, Rts. 5 & 20, Seneca Falls, N.Y. 13148.	Ms. Amy Walters	(315) 568-5893
46	Steuben County Office for the Aging, c/o The Infirmary, P.O. Box 631, Bath, N.Y. 14810.	Ms. Linda Tetor	(607) 776-7651
47	Suffolk County Office for the Aging, 65 Jetson Lane, Central Islip, N.Y. 11722.	Mr. Frank C. Trotta	(516) 348-5313
48	Sullivan County Office for the Aging, County Government Center, 100 N. St., Monticello, N.Y. 12701.	Mr. James J. Galligan	(914) 794-3000
49	Tioga County Office for Aging, 231 Main St., Oswego, N.Y. 13827.	Ms. Jean Hefft	(607) 687-4120
50	Tompkins County Office for Aging, 320 N. Tioga St., City Court House, Ithaca, N.Y. 14850.	Ms. Margaret Harding	(607) 274-5427
51	Ulster County Office for the Aging, 240-244 Fair St., Box 1800, Kingston, N.Y. 12401.	Ms. Patricia P. Pine	(914) 331-9300

NEW YORK—Continued

PSA	Area agency address	Director and telephone number
52	Warren/Hamilton Counties Office for the Aging, Warren County Municipal Center, Lake George, N.Y. 12845.	Mr. Louis Spelman, Jr., ...(518) 761-6347
53	Washington County Office for the Aging, Grays Corners Road, P.O. Box 58, Whitehall, N.Y. 12887.	Ms. Muriel Eckhard . . . .(518) 499-2468
54	Wayne County Area Agency on Aging, Turnpike Rd., P.O. Box 7336, Route 31 West, Lyons, N.Y. 14489.	Mr. Robert Lindner . . . .(315) 946-4163
55	Westchester County Office for the Aging, 214 Central Ave., room 938, White Plains, N.Y. 10601.	Ms. Mae Carpenter . . . .(914) 682-3045
56	Wyoming County Office for the Aging, 76 North Main St., Warsaw, N.Y. 14569.	Mr. Martin D. Mucher . . . . . .(716) 786-3144
57	Yates County Area Agency on Aging, 5 Collins Avenue, Penn Yan, N.Y. 14527.	Mr. Foster Van Duser . . . . . .(315) 536-2368
60	New York City Department for the Aging, 2 Lafayette St., New York, N.Y. 10007.	Ms. Janet Sainer . . . .(212) 577-0848
61	St. Regis-Mohawk Office for the Aging, St. Regis-Mohawk Indian Reservation, Hogansburg, N.Y. 13655.	Ms. Louise Brown . . . .(518) 358-2272
62	Seneca Nation of Indians Office for the Aging, 1500 Route 438, Irving, N.Y. 14081.	Ms. Roxanne Ray . . . .(716) 532-5777
63	Seneca County Office for the Aging, P.O. Box 480, Routes 5 and 20, Seneca Falls, N.Y. 13148.	Ms. Amy Walters . . . .(315) 568-5893

NORTH CAROLINA

(Federal Region IV)

STATE AGENCY ON AGING

Elaine Stoops, Assistant Secretary
DIVISION ON AGING
1985 Umpstead Dr. - Kirby Bldg.
Raleigh, North Carolina 27603
(919) 733-3983

AREA AGENCIES

PSA	Area agency address	Director and telephone number
1A	Southwestern North Carolina Planning and Economic Development Commission, P.O. Box 850, Bryson City, N.C. 28713.	Ms. Mary Barker . . . .(704) 488-9211
2B	Land of Sky Regional Council (Region B), 25 Heritage Dr., Asheville, N.C. 28806.	Ms. Joan B. Tuttle . . . .(704) 254-8131
3C	Isothermal Planning and Development Commission (Region C), 101 West Court St., P.O. Box 841, Rutherfordton, N.C. 28139.	Ms. Diane Padgett . . . .(704) 287-2281
4D	Region D Council of Governments, P.O. Box 1820, Executive Arts Building, Furman Rd., Boone, N.C. 28607.	Ms. Barbara Barghothi . . . . .(704) 264-5558
5E	Western Piedmont Council of Governments, (Region E), 30 Third St., NW., Hickory, N.C. 28601.	Ms. Mary Ann Squire . . . . . .(704) 322-9191
6F	Centralina Council of Governments, (Region F), 1300 Baxter St., P.O. Box 35008, Charlottetown Center, Charlotte, N.C. 28235.	Ms. Sue Archer . . . .(704) 372-2416
7G	Piedmont Triad Council of Governments, Kroger Center, Wilmington Bldg., Suite 201, 2216 West Meadowview Rd., Greensboro, N.C. 27407.	Ms. Lynn M. Perrin . . . .(919) 294-4950

NORTH CAROLINA—Continued

PSA	Area agency address	Director and telephone number
8H	Pee Dee Council of Governments, (Region H), 302 Leak St., P.O. Drawer 1417, Rockingham, N.C. 28379.	Ms. Karen Coble ....(919) 895-6306
9J	Triangle J Council of Governments, P.O. Box 12276, 100 Park Dr., Research Triangle Park, N.C. 27709.	Mr. David M. Moser ....(919) 549-0551
10K	Kerr Tar Regional Council of Governments, (Region K), 238 Orange St., P.O. Box 709, Henderson, N.C. 27536.	Mr. Steven Norwood ....(919) 492-8561
11L	Region L Council of governments, 1309 South Wesleyan Blvd., P.O. Box 2748, Rocky Mount, N.C. 27802.	Ms. Zelma Hillsman ....(919) 446-0411
12M	Region M Council of Governments, 130 Gillespie Street, P.O. Drawer 1510, Fayetteville, N.C. 28302.	Ms. Margaret Hardee ......(919) 323-4191
13N	Lumber River Council of Governments, (Region N), 4721 Fayetteville Road, P.O. Drawer 1529, Lumberton, N.C. 28359.	Ms. Betty Rising ....(919) 738-8104
14O	Cape Fear Council of Governments, (Region O), 321 North Front Street, P.O. Box 1491, Wilmington, N.C. 28402.	Ms. Jerry Ramsey ....(919) 763-0191
15P	Nuese River Council of Governments (Region P), 1404 Neuse Boulevard, P.O. Box 1717, New Bern, N.C. 28560.	Ms. Ann Holton ....(919) 638-3185
16Q	Mid-East Development Commission, (Region Q), 1 Harding Square, P.O. Box 1787, Washington, N.C. 27889.	Ms. Louisa Cox ....(919) 946-8043
17R	Albemarle Regional Planning and Development Commission, (Region R), P.O. Box 646, Hertford, N.C. 27944.	Mr. Lee Riddick ....(919) 426-5753
18I	Northwest Piedmont Council of Governments (Region I), 280 South Liberty St., Winston-Salem, N.C. 27101.	Ms. Rodessa Mitchell ......(919) 722-9346

NORTH DAKOTA*

(Federal Region VIII)

State Agency on Aging

Larry Brewster, Administrator
AGING SERVICES
Department of Human Services
State Capitol Building
Bismarck, North Dakota 58505
(701) 224-2577

*The State of North Dakota serves as a single planning and service area.

OHIO

(Federal Region V)

STATE AGENCY ON AGING

Joyce Chapple, Executive Director
DEPARTMENT ON AGING
50 West Broad Street – 9th Floor
Columbus, Ohio 43215
(614) 466–5500

AREA AGENCIES

PSA	Area agency address	Director and telephone number
1	Council on Aging of the Cincinnati Area, 601 Provident Bank Bldg., 7th and Vine, Cincinnati, Ohio 45202.	Mr. William Bogart . . . .(513) 721–1025
2	Area Agency on Aging, PSA 2, 184 Salem Ave., Dayton, Ohio 45406.	Mr. Doug McGarry . . . .(513) 225–3027
3	PSA 3 Area Agency on Aging, 311 Bldg., suite 201, 311 E. Market Street, Lima, Ohio 45801.	Dr. Harold K. Dahill . . . .(419) 222–7723
4	Area Office on Aging of Northwestern Ohio, Inc., Executive Office Bldg., 2155 Arlington Ave., Toledo, Ohio 43609.	Ms. Billie Sewell-Johnson . . .(419) 382–0624
5	District 5 Area Agency on Aging, 50 Blymer Ave., P.O. Box 966, Mansfield, Ohio 44901.	Ms. Caroline Ford . . . .(419) 524–4144
6	Central Ohio Area Agency on Aging, 272 S. Gift St., Columbus, Ohio 43215.	Ms. Jane L. Taylor . . . .(614) 222–7250

7	Area Agency on Aging, District 7, Inc., P.O. Box 978, Rio Grande College, Rio Grande, Ohio 45674.	Mr. Richard Leblanc	(614) 245-5306
8	Buckeye Hills-Hocking Valley Regional Development District, suite 410, St. Clair Bldg., 216 Putnam St., Marietta, Ohio 45750.	Ms. Cindy Farson	(614) 374-9436
9	Area Agency on Aging, Region 9, Box 429, 117 S. 11th St., Cambridge, Ohio 43725.	Ms. Evelyn Brockwell	(614) 439-4478
10A	Western Reserve Area Agency on Aging, Marion Bldg., room 512, 1276 W. 3d St., Cleveland, Ohio 44113.	Ms. Audrey Spencer	(216) 443-7560
10B	Area Office on Aging, 470 Grant St., Akron, Ohio 44311.	Mr. Joseph Ruby	(216) 376-9172
11	District 11 Area Agency on Aging, Ohio One Bldg., 25 E. Boardman St., Youngstown, Ohio 44503.	Ms. Martha Murphy	(216) 746-2938

OKLAHOMA

(Federal Region VI)

STATE AGENCY ON AGING

Roy Keen, Supervisor
SPECIAL UNIT ON AGING
Department of Human Services
P.O. Box 25352
Oklahoma City, Oklahoma 73125
(405) 521-2281

AREA AGENCIES

PSA	Area agency address	Director and telephone number
1	Grand Gateway EDA-Area Agency on Aging, P.O. Box 330, 1105 W. Canadian, Vinita, Okla. 74301.	Mr. Jim Mullin .... (918) 256-6478
2	EODD Area Agency on Aging, 800 West Okmulgee, P.O. Box 1376, Muskogee, Okla. 74402.	Ms. Lou Stackler .... (918) 682-7891
3	KEDDO Area Agency on Aging, Highway 2, North, P.O. Box 638, Wilburton, Okla. 74578.	Ms. Kay Langham .... (918) 465-2367
4	SODA Area Agency on Aging, P.O. Box 848, 16 'E' St., SW., Admore, Okla. 73401.	Mr. Marshall Collier .... (405) 226-2250
5	COEDD Area Agency on Aging, 400 N. Bell, Shawnee, Okla. 74801.	Ms. Sandra Washburn ...... (405) 273-6410
6	Tulsa Area Agency on Aging, 200 Civic Center, room 336, Tulsa, Okla. 74103.	Mr. Boyd Talley .... (918) 529-7688

7	NODA Area Agency on Aging, 3201 Sante Fe Trail, Enid, Okla. 73701.	Ms. Jessie Washington	(405) 237-4810
8	Areawide Agency on Aging, Inc., P.O. Box 1474, 125 Northwest 5th St., Oklahoma City, Okla. 73102.	Ms. Charlotte Heard	(405) 236-2426
9	ASCOG Area Agency on Aging, 802 Main St., P.O. Box 1647, Duncan, Okla. 73534.	Ms. Blaine Smith	(405) 252-0595
10	SWODA Area Agency on Aging, 802 Main, P.O. Box 1647, Burns Flat, Okla. 73534.	Mr. Jim Boyd	(405) 562-4886
11	OEDA Area Agency on Aging, 330 Douglas Ave., P.O. Box 668, Beaver, Okla. 73932.	Mr. John Trued	(405) 625-4531

OREGON

(Federal Region X)

STATE AGENCY ON AGING

Richard Ladd, Administrator
SENIOR SERVICES DIVISION
313 Public Service Building
Salem, Oregon 97310
(503) 378–4728

AREA AGENCIES

PSA	Area agency address	Director and telephone number
1	District 1, Area Agency on Aging, 116 Gower St., P.O. Box 488, Cannon Beach, Oreg. 97110.	Mr. Donald M. Fields ......(503) 436–1156
2A1	Clackamas Area Agency on Aging, 807 Main Street, Oregon City, Oreg. 97045.	Ms. Patricia Lyon ....(503) 655–8200
2A2	Columbia Council of Senior Citizens, Inc., 11 Plaza, P.O. Box 141, ST Helens, Oreg. 97204.	Ms. Dorothy Churchill .....(503) 397–4000
2A3	Washington County Aging Program, Administration Bldg., NE 3d, P.O. Box 1297, Hillsboro, Oreg. 97123.	Ms. Mary Lou Ritter ....(503) 640–3489
2B	Aging Services Division, 426 SW Stark, 5th floor, B 160, Portland, Oreg. 97204.	Mr. James McConnell ......(503) 248–3646
3	Mid-Willamette Valley Senior Services Agency, 410 Senator Bldg., 220 High St., NE., Salem, Oreg. 97301.	Mr. Ed Sage ....(503) 371–1313

4	Senior and Disabled Adult Services, 155 SW Madison, No. 5, Corvallis, Oreg. 97333.	Ms. Betty Johnson	(503) 757–6851
5	District 5 Area Agency on Aging, 125 8th Ave. East, Eugene, Oreg. 97401.	Mr. Ted Stevens	(503) 687–4283
6	Douglas County Senior Services, 621 W. Madrone, Roseburg, Oreg. 97470.	Mr. John De Groot	(503) 440–3601
7	District 7 Area Agency on Aging, 170 S. Second St., Suite 204, Coos Bay, Oreg. 97420.	Ms. Connie Croy	(503) 756–2563
8	District 8 Area Agency on Aging, Rouge Valley Council of Governments, 155 S. 2d St., room 200, P.O. Box 3275, Central Point, Oreg. 97502.	Mr. Don Bruland	(503) 664–6674
9	Mid-Columbia Area Agency on Aging, P.O. Box 988, 700 Union St., Room 233, The Dalles, Oreg. 97058.	Ms. Sally Sirrine	(503) 298–4101
10	Central Oregon Council on Aging, 1345 NW Wall St., Bend, Oreg. 97701.	Mr. Terry Lynch	(503) 389–3311
11	Klamath Basin Senior Citizens Council, 2045 Arthur St., Klamath Falls, Oreg. 97601.	Ms. Kathy Hundley	(503) 882–4098
12	East Central Oregon Association of Counties, Area Agency on Aging, 17 SW Frazer, P.O. Box 1207, Pendleton, Oreg. 97801.	Mr. Rollin Reynolds	(503) 276–6732
13	HELP, Inc., 104 Elm St., LaGrande, Oreg. 97850.	Mr. Dennis Naughton	(503) 963–3186
14A	Malheur Council on Aging, Box 937, 1309 N.W. 16th Ave., Ontario, Oreg. 97914.	Ms. Sherri Massongill	(503) 889–7651
14B	Harney County Senior Citizens, Inc., 17 South Alder St., Burns, Oreg. 97720.	Ms. Phyllis Lissman	(503) 573–6024

PENNSYLVANIA

(Federal Region III)

STATE AGENCY ON AGING

Linda Rhodes, Secretary
DEPARTMENT OF AGING
231 State Street
Harrisburg, Pennsylvania 17101–1195
(717) 783–1550

AREA AGENCIES

PSA	Area agency address	Director and telephone number
1	Erie County Area Agency on Aging, Greater Erie Community Action Committee, 18 West 9th St., Erie, Pa. 16501.	Ms. Elaine Clyburn . . . .(814) 459–4581
2	Active Aging Inc., 1034 Park Ave., Meadville, Pa. 16335.	Ms. Pauline Mooney . . . .(814) 336–1792
3	North Central Pennsylvania Office of Human Services, 108 Center Street, P.O. Box A, Ridgway, Pa. 15853.	Mr. William Orzechowski . . .(814) 776–2191
4	Beaver County Office on Aging, 599 Market St. W.B., Beaver, Pa. 15009.	Mr. R. Brandon James . . . . .(412) 728–5700
5	Aging Services, Inc. of Indiana County, 201 Airport Offices and Professional Center, R.D. 3, Indiana, Pa. 15701.	Ms. Carole A. Ling . . . .(412) 349–4500
6	Allegheny County Area Agency on Aging, 1400 Arrot Bldg., 401 Wood St., Pittsburgh, Pa. 15222.	Ms. Kathryn Ann Butchko . .(412) 355–4349
7	Westmoreland County Area Agency on Aging, 2482 South Grande Blvd., Greensburg, Pa. 15601.	Mr. Ray DuCoeur . . . .(412) 836–1111

8	Southwestern Pennsylvania Area Agency on Aging, Eastgate 8, Monessen, Pa. 15062.	Ms. Holly Lange	(412) 684-9000
9	Area Agency on Aging of Somerset County, 147 East Union St., P.O. Box 960, Somerset, Pa. 15501.	Mr. Arthur N. DiLoreto	(814) 443-2681
10	Cambria County Area Agency on Aging, R.D. 3, Box 614, Lovell R.D., Ebensburg, Pa. 15931.	Mr. John Waterstram	(814) 472-5580
11	Blair Senior Services, Inc., 1404 Eleventh Avenue, Altoona, Pa. 16601.	Mr. David M. Slat	(814) 946-1235
12	Huntingdon/Bedford/Fulton Area Agency on Aging, 240 Wood Street, P.O. Box 46, Bedford, Pa. 15522	Mr. R. Alan Smith	(814) 623-8149
13	Centre County Area Agency on Aging, Willowbank Bldg., Homes and Valentine Sts. Bellefonte, Pa. 16823.	Mrs. Cynthia Edvar	(814) 355-6716
14	Bi-County Office on Aging (Lycoming/Clinton), P.O. Box 770, 352 East Water St., Lock Haven, Pa. 17745.	Ms. Virginia Crosby	(717) 748-8665
15	Columbia/Montour Area Agency on Aging, 243 West Main St., Bloomsburg, Pa. 17815.	Mr. Robert Levan	(717) 784-9272
16	Northumberland County Area Agency on Aging, R.D. #1, Box 943, State Route 225, Shamokin, Pa. 17872.	Mr. Nicholas E. Bahner	(717) 644-4545
17	Union/Snyder County Office on Aging, 116 N. Second St., Lewisburg, Pa. 17837.	Ms. Farida Zaid	(717) 837-0675
18	Mifflin-Juniata Area Agency on Aging, Inc., P.O. Box 750, Buena Vista Circle, Lewistown, Pa. 17044.	Ms. Carlene Hack	(717) 242-0315
19	Franklin County Office for the Aging, Franklin County Farm Lane, Chambersburg, Pa. 17201.	Mr. Robert Keith	(717) 263-2153
20	Adams County Area Agency on Aging, 100 North Stratton St., Gettysburg, Pa. 17013.	Mr. Steven Niebler	(717) 334-9296
21	Cumberland County Office on Aging, 35 East High St., Carlisle, Pa. 17013.	Ms. Judy Shuey	(717) 243-8442
22	Perry County Office for the Aging, Courthouse Annex, South Carlisle St., New Bloomfield, Pa. 17068.	Ms. Susan McAllister	(717) 582-2131

PENNSYLVANIA—Continued

PSA	Area agency address	Director and telephone number
23	Dauphin County Area Agency on Aging, 25 S. Front St., Harrisburg, Pa. 17101-2025.	Mr. Lewis L. Crippen . . . .(717) 255-2790
24	Lebanon County Area Agency on Aging, 710 Maple St., room 209, Senior Center, Lebanon, Pa. 17042.	Mr. Michael Kristovensky . . .(717) 273-9262
25	York County Area Agency on Aging, 141 West Market St., York, Pa. 17401.	Ms. Kathleen Boas . . . .(717) 771-9610
26	Lancaster County Office on Aging, 50 North Duke St., Lancaster, Pa. 17603-1881.	Ms. Patricia Mann . . . .(717) 299-7979
27	Chester County Services for Senior Citizens, 14 East Biddle St., West Chester, Pa. 19380.	Ms. Meg Woodlief . . . .(215) 431-6350
28	Montgomery County Office on Aging and Adult Sves., Montgomery County Court House, Norristown, Pa. 19404.	Mr. Edward Keenan . . . .(215) 278-3601
29	Bucks County Area Agency on Aging, 30 E. Oklahoma Ave., Doylestown, Pa. 18901.	Ms. Margaret O'Neill . . . . . .(215) 348-0510
30	Delaware County Services for the Aging, Second and Orange Sts., Government Center, Media, Pa. 19063	Mr. John Bauer . . . .(215) 891-4455
31	Philadelphia Corporation for Aging, 111 North Broad St., Philadelphia, Pa. 19107.	Mr. Rodney Williams . . . .(215) 496-0520
32	Berks County Area Agency on Aging, 15 South 8th St., Reading, Pa. 19602.	Ms. Barbara Coffin . . . .(215) 378-8808
33	Lehigh County Area Agency on Aging, Courthouse Annex, 523 Hamilton St., Allentown, Pa. 18101.	Mr. Peter Johnstone . . . .(215) 820-3248
34	Northampton County Area Agency on Aging Gracedale-South West-Ground, Gracedale Ave., Nazareth, Pa. 18064.	Mr. John Mehler . . . .(215) 759-7970
35	Wayne/Pike Agency on Aging, Pike County Program Office, 106 Broad St., Milford, Pa. 18337.	Ms. Linda Peifer . . . .(717) 296-7813
36	Area Agency on Aging for the Counties of Bradford, Sullivan, Susquehanna, and Tioga, 701 Main St., Towanda, Pa. 18848.	Mr. William Girtman . . . .(717) 265-6121
37	Luzerne/Wyoming Counties Bureau for the Aging, 111 North Pennsylvania Blvd., Wilkes-Barre, Pa. 18701.	Mr. Charles Adams . . . .(717) 822-1158

38	Lackawanna County Area Agency on Aging, 200 Adams Ave., Scranton, Pa. 18503.	Mr. John T. Nalevanko	(717) 963-6740
39	Carbon County Area Agency on Aging, Court House Annex, P.O. Box 251, Jim Thorpe, Pa. 18229.	Mr. Albert Petrole	(717) 325-2726
40	Schuylkill County Area Agency on Aging, 13-15 North Centre St., Pottsville, Pa. 17901.	Ms. Margaret Kralick	(717) 622-3103
41	Clearfield County Area Agency on Aging, Inc., 211 Ogden Ave., P.O. Box 558, Clearfield, Pa. 16830.	Mr. John Kordish	(814) 765-2696
42	Jefferson County Area Agency on Aging, Jefferson County Service Center, R.D. 5, Brookville, Pa. 15825.	Ms. Laura Mae Baker	(814) 849-3096
43	Experience, Inc., Area Agency on Aging, 514 West Third Avenue, P.O. Box 886, Warren, Pa. 16365.	Mr. Allen R. Roberts	(814) 726-1700
44	Venango County Area Agency on Aging, P.O. Box 1130, Franklin, Pa. 16323.	Ms. Christine Ross	(814) 437-6871
45	Armstrong County Area Agency on Aging, 200 Oak Ave., Kittanning, Pa. 16201.	Ms. Dorothy Dailey	(412) 548-7516
46	Lawrence County Area Agency on Aging, 20 South Mercer St., New Castle, Pa. 16101.	Ms. Roberta Taylor	(412) 658-5661
47	Mercer County Area Agency on Aging, Human Services Complex, 120 S. Diamond St., Mercer, Pa. 16137.	Ms. Anne Marie Spiardi	(412) 662-3800
48	Monroe County Area Agency on Aging, 62 Analomink St., East Stroudsburg, Pa. 18301.	Ms. Dorothy Kaufman	(717) 424-5290
49	Clarion County Area Agency on Aging, 12 Grant St., Clarion, Pa. 16214.	Ms. Carolyn Lambert	(814) 226-4640
50	Butler County Area Agency on Aging, Morgan Management Bldg., 165 Brugh Ave., Suite 321, Butler, Pa. 16001.	Mr. Harold Beazell	(412) 282-3008

RHODE ISLAND

(Federal Region I)

STATE AGENCY ON AGING

Adelaide Luber, Director
DEPARTMENT OF ELDERLY AFFAIRS
79 Washington Street
Providence, Rhode Island 02903
(401) 277-2858

*The State of Rhode Island serves as a single planning and service area.

SOUTH CAROLINA

(Federal Region IV)

STATE AGENCY ON AGING

Ruth Seigler, Director
COMMISSION ON AGING
915 Main Street
Columbia, South Carolina 29201
(803) 783-3203

AREA AGENCIES

PSA	Area agency address	Director and telephone number
1	Appalachian Council of Governments, P.O. Drawer 6668, 50 Grand Avenue, Greenville, S.C. 29606.	Mr. Michael Stocnea ....(803) 242-9733
2A	Abbeville County Council on Governments, Center Drive, P.O. Box 117, Abbeville, S.C. 29602.	Mr. George Buell ....(803) 459-4511
2E	Edgefield Senior Citizens Council, 400 Church St., P.O. Box 510, Edgefield, S.C. 29824.	Ms. Fairey English ....(803) 637-5326
2G	Greenwood County Council on Aging, 123 Bailey Circle, P.O. Box 997, Greenwood, S.C., 29646.	Ms. Lila Hanley ....(803) 223-0164
2L	Laurens County Council for Senior Citizens Programs, P.O. Box 777, Laurens, S.C. 29360	Ms. Anne Wardlaw ....(803) 984-4572
2M	McCormick County Senior Citizens Programs, 407 Augusta ST., P.O. 684, McCormick, S.C. 29835	Ms. Leila McMillan ....(803) 465-2626

—Continued

PSA	Area agency address	Director and telephone number
2S	Saluda County Council on Aging, 104 W. Church St., P.O. Box 507, Saluda, S.C. 29138.	Ms. Reba Bodie . . . .(803) 445–2175
3	Catawba Regional Planning Council, 100 Dave Lyle Blvd., Suite 300, P.O. Box 450, Rock Hill, S.C. 29730.	Ms. Janice Hoak . . . .(803) 327–9041
4	Central Midlands Regional Planning Council, 800 Dutch Square Blvd., NO. 155, Columbia, S.C. 29210.	Ms. Sue Scally . . . .(803) 798–1243
5	Lower Savannah Council of Governments, Highway 302 North, P.O. Box 850, Aiken, S.C. 29801.	Ms. Connie Shade . . . .(803) 649–7981
6	Santee-Lynches Regional Council. Box 1837, Sumter, S.. 29150.	Ms. Darlene Threatt . . . .(803) 775–7382
7	Pee Dee Council of Governments, P.O. Box 5719, Florence–Darlington Highway, Florence, S.C. 29502.	Cynthia B. Moore . . . .(803) 669–3138
8	Waccamaw Regional Planning Council, 1001 Front Street, P.O. Drawer 419, Georgetown, S.C. 29440.	Ms. Michelle Hudson . . . . . .(803) 546–8502
9	Trident Area Agency on Aging, P.O. Box 2696, 1069 King St., Charleston, S.C. 29403.	Ms. Sandra Clair . . . .(803) 723–1676
10	Low Country Council of Governments, Interstate 95; U.S. 17, P.O. Box 98, Yemeassee, S.C. 29945.	Sandy Nutting . . . .(803) 726–5536

SOUTH DAKOTA*

(Federal Region VIII)

State Agency on Aging

Michael Vogel, Executive Director
OFFICE OF ADULT SERVICES AND AGING
700 North Illinois Street
Kneip Building
Pierre, South Dakota 57501
(605) 773-3656

*The State of South Dakota serves as a single planning and service area.

TENNESSEE

(Federal Region IV)

STATE AGENCY ON AGING

Emily Wiseman, Executive Director
COMMISSION ON AGING
Suite 201
706 Church Street
Nashville, Tennessee 37219–5573
(615) 741–2056

AREA AGENCIES

PSA	Area agency address	Director and telephone number
	First Tennessee Area Agency on Aging, 207 North Boone, Suite 800, Johnson City, Tenn. 37601.	Ms. Patricia Brown ....(615) 928–0224
2	Area Agency on Aging, East Tennessee Human Resource Agency, P.O. Box 14428, 6712 Deane Hill Dr., Knoxville, Tenn. 37939.	Mr. Aaron Bradley ....(615) 691–2551
3	CARCOG/Southeast Tennessee Development District, 216 West 8th St., Suite 300,Chattanooga, Tenn. 37402.	Mr. Viston Taylor ....(615) 266–5781
4	Upper Cumberland Plng. & Svc. Area, 1225 Burgess Falls Rd., Cookeville, Tenn. 38501.	Ms. Nancy Peace ....(615) 432–4111
5	Mid-Cumberland Development District, 211 Union St., Box 233 Stahlman Bldg. 7th Floor, Nashville, Tenn. 37201	Mr. Rick Fowlkes ....(615) 259–5491
6	South Central Tennessee Development District, 815 South Main, P.O. Box 1346, Columbia, Tenn. 38401.	Mr. Bob Lundquist ....(615) 381–2040

7	Northwest Planning & Service Area, P.O. Box 63, Weldon Dr., Martin, Tenn. 38237.	Mr. Paul D. Steele ....(901) 587–4215
8	Southwest Tennessee Development District, 416 East Lafayette St., Jackson, Tenn. 38301.	Ms. Ann Lewis ....(901) 422–4041
9	Delta Commission on Aging, City Hall, room 419, 125 N. Mid-Amer Hall, Memphis, Tenn. 38103.	Mr. Robert McFalls ....(901) 528–2600

TEXAS

(Federal Region VI)

STATE AGENCY ON AGING

O.P. (Bob) Bobbitt, Director
DEPARTMENT ON AGING
P.O. Box 12786 Capitol Station
1949 IH 35, South Austin, Texas 78741–3702
(512) 444–2727

AREA AGENCIES

PSA	Area agency address	Director and telephone number
1	Panhandle Region Planning Council Area Agency on Aging, P.O. Box 9257, 2736 W. 10th, Amarillo, Tex. 79105.	Mr. Mike McQueen ....(806) 372–3381
2	South Plains Association of Governments, 1323 58th, Lubbock, Tex. 79408.	Mr. Robert Marshall ....(806) 762–8721
3	NORTEX Regional Planning Commission, P.O. Box 5144, 2101 Kemp Blvd., Wichita Falls, Tex. 76307.	Ms. Lila Reed ....(817) 322–5281

TEXAS—Continued

PSA	Area agency address	Director and telephone number
4A	North Central Texas Council of Government—Area Agency on Aging, 616 Six Flags Dr., Center Point 2, P.O. Drawer COG, Arlington Tex. 76005-5888.	Ms. Wilma Morgan ....(817) 461-3300
4B	Community Council of Greater Dallas, 2121 Main Street, Suite 500, Dallas, Tex. 75201.	Mr. Norman L. Moorehead ..(214) 741-5851
4C	Tarrant County Area Agency on Aging, 201 E. Ninth St., Fort Worth, Tex. 76102.	Ms. Victoria Klinzing ......(817) 335-3473
5	Ark-Tex Area COG, 911 Loop 151, Suite 100, Bldg. A, P.O. Box 5307, Texarkana, Tex. 75507.	Ms. Beverely Cherney Pearson ....(501) 774-3481
6	East Texas Area Agency on Aging, 3800 Stone Rd., Kilgore, Tex. 75662.	Mr. Claude I. Andrews .....(214) 984-8641
7	West Central Texas Area Agency on Aging, 1025 East North 10th, P.O. Box 3195, Abilene, Tex. 79604.	Dr. Lewis E. Lemmond .....(915) 672-8544
8	West Texas COG Area Agency on Aging, 123 Pioneer Plaza, The Cientres, El Paso, Tex. 79901.	Ms. Rosemary Castillo .....(915) 541-4681
9	Permian Basin, Reg. Plng. Comm., P.O. Box 6391, Midland, Tex. 79711.	Mr. Wm. E. (Bill) Smith .....(915) 563-1061
10	Concho Valley Area Agency on Aging, P.O. Box 60050, 5002 Knickerbocker Rd., San Angelo, Tex. 76906.	Ms. Betty Ford ....(915) 944-9666
11	Heart of Texas Council of Governments—Area Agency on Aging, 320 Franklin Ave., Waco, Tex. 76701.	Ms. Hazel Limback ....(817) 756-6631
12	Capital Area Agency on Aging, 2520 Interstate Highway 355, South, suite 100, Austin, Tex. 78704.	Ms. Andriette Short ....(512) 443-7653

13	Brazos Valley Dev. Council Area Agency on Aging, P.O. Drawer 4128, Bryan, Tex. 77805-4128.	Ms. Roberta Lindquist	(713) 822-7421
14	Deep East Texas Area Agency on Aging, 271 East Lamar, P.O. Drawer 1170, Jasper, Tex. 75951.	Ms. Martha Jones	(713) 384-5704
15	South East Texas Regional Planning Commission—Area Agency on Aging, 3800 Highway 365, suite 113, Port Arthur, Tex. 77640.	Ms. Joyce Philen	(713) 727-2384
16A	Houston-Galveston Area Agency on Aging, 3550 Timmons, Suite 500, P.O. Box 22777, Houston, Tex. 77227.	Ms. Jackie Martin	(713) 627-3200
16B	Houston-Harris County Area Agency on Aging, 806 Main, 3rd Floor, P.O. Box 1562, Houston, Tex. 77251.	Ms. Antoinette A. Samuel	(713) 236-7700
17	Golden Crescent Regional Planning Commission—Area Agency on Aging, P.O. Box 2028, Victoria Regional Airport Bldg. 102, Victoria, Tex. 77902.	Ms. Clara Prater	(512) 578-1587
18A	Alamo Area Agency on Aging, 118 Broadway, suite 400, San Antonio, Tex. 78205.	Mr. Frank Adamo	(512) 225-5201
18B	Bexar County Area Agency on Aging, 118 Broadway, suite 400, San Antonia, Tex. 78205.	Ms. Minnie R. Williams	(512) 225-5201
19	South Texas Area Agency on Aging, 600 South Sandman, P.O. Box 2187, Laredo, Tex. 78041.	Ms. Andres Smith	(512) 722-3995
20	Costal Bend Area Agency on Aging, 2910 Leopard, P.O. Box 9909, Corpus Christi, Tex. 78408.	Mr. Ivan Arceneaux	(512) 883-5743
21	Lower Rio Grande Valley Area Agency on Aging, 4900 N. 23rd St., McAllen, Tex. 78502.	Mr. Leobardo Garcia	(512) 682-3481
22	Texoma Area Agency on Aging, 10000 Grayson Dr., Denison, Tex. 75020.	Ms. Janis Gray	(214) 786-2955
23	Central Texas Council of Government—Area Agency on Aging, 302 East Central, P.O. Box 729, Belton, Tex. 76513.	Ms. Margareta Williams	(817) 939-1886.
24	Middle Rio Grande Valley—Area Agency on Aging, 403 East Nopal, P.O. Box 1199, Carrizo Spring, Tex. 78834.	Ms. Estella Hernandez	(512) 876-3533.

UTAH

(Federal Region VIII)

STATE AGENCY ON AGING

Robert K. Ward, Director
DIVISION OF AGING AND ADULT SERVICES
Department of Social Services
150 West North Temple
Box 45500
Salt Lake City, Utah 84145–0500
(801) 533–6422

AREA AGENCIES

PSA	Area agency address	Director and telephone number
1	Bear River Area Agency on Aging, 170 North Main Street, Logan, Utah 84321.	Ms. Susan Amman ....(801) 752–7242
2A	Weber County Department of Aging and Volunteer Services, 2650 Lincoln, Rm. 268, Ogden, Utah 84401.	Mr. Kenneth Bradshaw .....(801) 399–8840
2B	Salt Lake County Aging Services, 2001 South State, Ste. S-1500, Salt Lake City, Utah 84190–2300.	Ms. Shauna O'Neil ....(801) 468–2454
2C	Davis County Council on Aging, Davis County Courthouse Annex, 28 East State Street, P.O. Box 618, Farmington, Utah 84025.	Ms. Alice J. Johnson ....(801) 451–3370
2T	Tooele Area Agency on Aging, 59 East Vine, P.O. Box 477, Tooele, Utah 84074.	Mr. Edwin Dymock ....(801) 882–2870

3	Mountainland Area Agency on Aging, 2545 North Canyon Road, Provo, Utah 84604–5906.	Mr. Ted Livingston	(801) 377–2262
4	Aging Services District IV, P.O. Box 788, Sevier County Courthouse, Richfield, Utah 84701.	Mr. Ross Bumgardner	(801) 896–9222
5	Five County Area Agency on Aging, 237 N. Bluff, P.O. Box 1500, St. George, Utah 84770.	Mr. Bob Rasmussen	(801) 673–3548
6A	Uintah Basin Area Agency on Aging, 120 South 100 East, #43–4, Roosevelt, Utah 84066.	Mr. Gerald Conley	(801) 722–4518
6C	Uintah County Area Agency on Aging, 155 South 100 West, Vernal, Utah 84078.	Mr. Ralph Siddoway	(801) 789–2169
7A	Southeast Utah Area Agency on Aging, Industrial Park, P.O. Drawer 1106, Prince, Utah 84501.	Mr. Mauchan Guymon	(801) 637–4268
7B	San Juan Area Agency on Aging, 117 So. Main, P.O. Box 9, Monticello, Utah 84535.	Mr. Rick Bailey	(801) 587–2231

VERMONT

(Federal Region I)

STATE AGENCY ON AGING

Joel Cook, Director
OFFICE ON AGING
103 South Main Street
Waterbury, Vermont 05676
(802) 241-2400

AREA AGENCIES

PSA	Area agency address	Director and telephone number
A	Champlain Valley Area Agency on Aging, Inc., 110 East Spring St., Winooski, Vt. 05404.	Ms. Mara Coven .... (802) 655-0084
B	Central Vermont Council on Aging, 18 South Main St., Barre, Vt. 05641.	Mr. Craig Hammond .... (802) 479-0531
C	Area Agency on Aging for Northeastern Vermont, 44 Main St., P.O. Box 640, St. Johnsbury, Vt. 05819.	Ms. Jean Denam .... (802) 748-5182
D	Southwestern Vermont Area Agency on Aging, 142 Merchants Row, Rutland, Vt. 05701.	Mr. John Campbell .... (802) 775-0486
E	Council on Aging for Southeastern Vermont, 139 Main Street, P.O. Box 818, Brattleboro, Vt. 05301.	Mr. James Matteau .... (802) 257-0569

VIRGINIA

(Federal Region III)

STATE AGENCY ON AGING

Wilda Ferguson, Commissioner
DEPARTMENT ON AGING
101 North 14th Street – 18th Floor
James Monroe Building
Richmond, Virginia 23219
(804) 225–2271

AREA AGENCIES

PSA	Area agency address	Director and telephone number
1	Mountain Empire Older Citizens Group, 330 Norton Rd., P.O. Box 1097, Wise, Va. 24293.	Ms. Marilyn Pace Maxwell . .(703) 328–2302
2	Appalachian Agency on Senior Citizens, Box S.V.C.C., Richlands, Va. 23641.	Ms. Diana Wallace . . . .(703) 964–4915
3	District III Governmental Cooperative, 305 S. Park St., Marion, Va. 24354.	Mr. Michael Guy . . . .(703) 783–8158
4	New River Valley Agency on Aging, 143 3d St., NW., Pulaski, Va. 24301.	Ms. Debbie H. Palmer . . . . . .(703) 980–8888
5	League of Older Americans, Inc., 706 Campbell Ave., SW., Roanoke, Va. 24016.	Mr. Glenn B. McKibben . . . .(703) 345–0451
6	Valley Program for Aging Services, 352 Pine Ave., P.O. Box 817, Waynesboro, Va. 22980.	Ms. Ann Bender . . . .(703) 949–7141

VIRGINIA—Continued

PSA	Area agency address	Director and telephone number
7	Shenandoah Area Agency on Aging, Inc., 15 North Royal Ave., Front Royal, Va. 22630.	Ms. Mary Spencer . . . .(703) 635-7141
8A	District Office on Aging, 2525 Mt. Vernon Ave., Unit 5, Alexandria, Va. 22301-1119.	Ms. Moya Atkinson . . . .(703) 838-4822
8B	Arlington Area Agency on Aging, 1801 N. George Mason Drive, Arlington, Va. 22207.	Ms. Terri Lynch . . . .(703) 558-2341
8C	Fairfax County Area Agency on Aging, 11212 Waples Mill Road, Fairfax, Va. 22030-6036.	Ms. Carla Pittman . . . .(703) 691-3384
8D	Loudoun County Area Agency on Aging, 115 Harrison St. NE., Leesburg, Va. 22075.	Ms. Ann Edwards . . . .(703) 777-0257
8E	Prince William Area Agency on Aging, 9252 Lee Ave., Manassas, Va. 22110.	Ms. Lin Wagener . . . .(703) 335-6400
9	Rappahannock-Rapidan Area Agency on Aging, 401 South Main St., Culpeper, Va. 22701.	Ms. Sallie Morgan . . . .(703) 825-6494
10	Jefferson Area Agency on Aging, 204 Lexington Ave., Charlottesville, Va. 22901.	Mr. Gordon Walker . . . .(804) 977-3444
11	Central Virginia Commission on Aging, Forest Hill Center, 2820 Linkhorne Dr., Lynchburg, Va. 24503.	Mr. T. C. Jones . . . .(804) 384-0372
12	Piedmont Seniors of Virginia, Inc., 827 Starling Ave., Martinsville, Va. 24112.	Ms. Alice Canupp . . . .(703) 632-6442
13	Lake County Commission on Aging, 1105 West Danville St., South Hill, Va. 23970.	Ms. Gay S. Currie . . . .(804) 447-7661
14	Piedmont Senior Resources, Area Agency on Aging, Piedmont Hospital Bldg., Room 228, P.O. Box 398, Burkeville, Va. 23922.	Mr. Ronald Dunn . . . .(804) 767-5588
15	Capital Area Agency on Aging, 316 E. Clay St., Richmond, Va. 23219.	Ms. Mary C. Payne . . . .(804) 648-8381
16	Rappahannock Area Agency on Aging, Inc., 204 Thompson Ave., Fredericksburg, Va. 22405.	Mr. Frank Beddow . . . .(703) 371-3375

17/18	Northern Neck–Middle Peninsula Area Agency on Aging, Virginia St., P.O. Box 610, Urbana, Va. 23175.	Mr. Allyn Gemerek	(804) 758–2386
19	Crater District Area Agency on Aging, 120 West Bank St., Petersburg, Va. 23803.	Mr. Richard Bull	(804) 732–7020
20	Southeastern Virginia Areawide Model Program, 7 Koger Executive Center, suite 100, Norfolk, Va. 23502.	Ms. Kathleen Donoghue	(804) 461–9481
21	Peninsula Agency on Aging, Inc., 13195 Warwick Blvd., Newport News, Va. 23602.	Mr. William Massey	(804) 874–2495
22	Eastern Shore Community Development Group, Inc., 54 Market St., P.O. Box 8, Onancock, Va. 23417.	Ms. Fay Lohr	(804) 787–3532

WASHINGTON

(Federal Region X)

STATE AGENCY ON AGING

Mr. Charles Reed, Assistant Secretary
AGING AND ADULT SERVICES ADMINISTRATION
Department of Social and Health Services
OB–44A
Olympia, Washington 98504
(206) 586–3768

AREA AGENCIES

PSA	Area agency address	Director and telephone number
1A	Olympic Area Agency on Aging, 2109 Summer Ave., room 203, Aberdeen, Wash. 98520.	Ms. Beverly Brice ....(206) 533–9385
1B	Olympic Area Agency on Aging, P.O. Box 1062, 820 Sheridan, 2d Floor, Port Townsend, Wash. 98368.	Ms. Beverly Brice ....(206) 385–2564
2	Northwest Washington Area Agency on Aging, 1000 Forest St., Courthouse Annex, Belingham, Wash. 98225.	Mr. Dewey Desler ....(206) 676–6749
3	Snohomish County Division of Aging, DHS, 1316 Wall, Everett, Wash. 98201.	Mr. Mike Manley ....(206) 259–9586
4	King County Area Agency on Aging, 110 Prefontaine Pl., Seattle, Wash. 98104.	Ms. Denise Klein ....(206) 625–4711
5	Pierce County Area Agency on Aging, 2401 35th St., Tacoma, Wash. 98409.	Ms. Pamela Fortin ....(206) 593–4828

6	Lewis/Mason/Thurston Area Agency on Aging, 529 South West 4th Ave., Olympia, Wash. 98501.	Mr. Dennis Mahar	(206) 786-5579
7	Southwest Washington Area Agency on Aging, 1703 Main Street, P.O. Box 425, Vancouver, Wash. 98666-0425.	Ms. Kamala Bremer	(206) 694-6577
8	North Central Area Agency on Aging, 1300 5th St., Wenatchee, Wash. 98801.	Mr. John B. Cottrell	(509) 662-1651
9	Yakima/Southeast Washington Area Agency on Aging, 2009 South 64th Ave., Yakima, Wash. 98903.	Mr. Greg Heartburg	(509) 575-4226
10	Yakima Indian Nation Area Agency on Aging, P.O. Box 151, Toppenish, Wash. 98948.	Mr. Doug Olney	(509) 865-5121
11	Eastern Washington Area Agency on Aging, West 1101 College Ave., room 365, Spokane, Wash. 99201-2096.	Mr. Nick Beamer	(509) 458-2509
12	Colville Confederated Tribes, P.O. Box 150, Nespelem, Wash. 99155.	Mr. Mal Tonasket	(509) 634-4761
13	Kitsap County Area Agency on Aging, Kitsap County Courthouse, 614 Division St., Port Orchard, Wash. 98366.	Ms. Gail Hiestand	(206) 876-7068

WEST VIRGINIA

(Federal Region III)

STATE AGENCY ON AGING

Susan Harman, Director
COMMISSION ON AGING
Holly Grove – State Capitol
Charleston, West Virginia 25305
(304) 348–3317

AREA AGENCIES

PSA	Area agency address	Director and telephone number
1	Region 1 Planning and Development Council, P.O. Box 1442, Princeton, W.Va. 24740.	Ms. Sharon Hondos . . . . . .(304) 425–9508
2	Region II Planning and Development Council, P.O. Box 939, 1221 6th Ave., Huntington, W.Va. 25712.	Mr. Jim Stone . . . .(304) 529–3357
3	Community Council of Kanawha Valley, 702½ Lee St. East, Box 2711, Charleston, W.Va. 25330.	Ms. Judy King . . . .(304) 340–3515
4	Eastern Highlands Area Agency on Aging, 500–B Main St., Summersville, W.Va. 26651.	Mr. Tim Bailes . . . .(304) 872–4970
5	Mid-Ohio Valley Regional Council, 925 Market St., P.O. Box 247, Parkersburg, W.Va. 26102.	Ms. Connie Farnsworth . . . .(304) 422–0522
6	Region VI Area Agency on Aging, 201 Deveny Bldg., Fairmont, W.Va. 26554.	Mr. Jon Hunter . . . .(304) 366–5693

7	Central West Virginia Area Agency on Aging, 5 S. Florida St., P.O. Box 186, Buckhannon, W.Va. 26201.	Ms. Evelyn Post	(304) 472-0395
8,9	Upper Potomac Area Agency on Aging, Airport Rd., P.O. Box 869, Petersburg, W.Va. 26847.	Mr. Art Trenton	(304) 257-1221
10/11	Northern Panhandle Area Agency on Aging, 2177 National Rd., Wheeling, W.Va. 26003.	Ms. Gaylene Miller	(304) 242-1800

WISCONSIN

(Federal Region V)

STATE AGENCY ON AGING

Donna McDowell, Director
BUREAU OF AGING
Division of Community Services
One West Wilson Street – Room 480
Madison, Wisconsin 53702
(608) 266–2536

AREA AGENCIES

PSA	Area agency address	Director and telephone number
1	Area Agency on Aging, District 1, 3601 Memorial Dr., Madison, Wis. 53704.	Mr. Arthur Hendrick ....(608) 249–0441
2A	Area Agency 2A, 1442 North Farwell, room 400, 2d floor, Milwaukee, Wis. 53702.	Mr. Fred Lindner ....(414) 272–8606
2B	Southeast Wisconsin Area Agency on Aging, W25S – N499 Grandview Blvd., Waukesha, Wis. 53188.	Ms. Helen A. Ramon ....(414) 521–5420
3	Lake Michigan-Winnebago Area Agency on Aging, 850–C Lombardi Ave., Green Bay, Wis. 54301.	Mr. Harry Collins ....(414) 465–1662
4	Western Wisconsin Area Agency on Aging, 505 Dewey St. S., Room 207, Eau Claire, Wis. 54701.	Mr. Troy Keeling ....(715) 836–4105
5	District VII Northern Central Area Agency on Aging, P.O. Box 1028, 1835 N. Stevens, Rhinelander, Wis. 54501.	Mr. Charles Arndt ....(715) 362–7800

WYOMING*

(Federal Region VIII)

STATE AGENCY ON AGING

Scott Sessions, Director
COMMISSION ON AGING
Hathaway Building - Room 139
Cheyenne, Wyoming 82002-0710
(307) 777-7986

*The State of Wyoming serves as a single planning service area.

AMERICAN SAMOA*

(Federal Region IX)

STATE AGENCY ON AGING

Tali Maae, Director
TERRITORIAL ADMINISTRATION ON AGING
Office of the Governor
Pago Pago, American Samoa 96799
011 (684) 633-1252

*Serves as a single planning and service area.

GUAM*

(Federal Region IX)

STATE AGENCY ON AGING

Dr. Laticia Espaldon, Director
PUBLIC HEALTH AND SOCIAL SERVICES
Government of Guam
Agana, Guam 96910

*Guam serves as a single planning and service area.

PUERTO RICO

(Federal Region II)

STATE AGENCY ON AGING

Pura Quesada Picó, Executive Director
GERICULTURE COMMISSION
Department of Social Services
P.O. Box 11398
Santurce, Puerto Rico 00910
(809) 721–3141 or 722–0225

AREA AGENCIES

PSA	Area agency address	Director and telephone number
1	Area Agency on Aging Aguadilla Region, Gericulture Regional Office, Box 126, Victoria Station, Aguadilla, P.R. 00605.	Mr. Pablo Badillo Roldán . . .(809) 891–1095
2	Area Agency on Aging Arecibo Region, Gericulture Regional Office, Calle Manuel Ruiz Gandia, No. 111, Edif. Metro Finance, Arecibo, P.R. 00612.	Ms. Olga Rodriguez . . . .(809) 878–4095
3	Area Agency on Aging Bayamon Region, Dr. Ferrer St., No. 4, Bayamón, P.R. 00691.	Mr. Jesús M. Alicea Sánchez .(809) 780–1073
4	Area Agency on Aging Caguas Region, Box 250, Barranquitas, P.R. 00618.	Ms. Zylma Colón . . . .(809) 857–2182
5	Area Agency on Aging Carolina Region, N–6 Benigno Garcia St., Este Carolina, P.R. 00630.	Mrs. Ada Quijano . . . .(809) 752–6142

6	Area Agency on Aging Guayama Region, Unión St., Casa Alcaldía, Salinas, P.R. 00751.	Mrs. Carmen Rodríguez	(809) 824–3060
7	Area Agency on Aging Humacao Region, 124–B Font Martelo St., Humacao, P.R. 00661.	Mrs. Alma Pagán	(809) 874–4130
8	Area Agency on Aging Mayagüez Region, Box 2721, Centro Cultural, Mayagüez, P.R. 00709.	Mrs. Lourdes Aquino	(809) 833–4536
9	Area Agency on Aging Ponce Region, Box 1540, H–W #13 Santaella St., Coamo, P.R. 00640.	Mrs. Nilda Zayas	(809) 825–2830
10	Area Agency on Aging San Juan, Centro Commercial Plaza 18, Roberto H. Todd Ave., 2d floor, Santurce, P.R. 00907.	Mrs. Manuelita Ortiz Aponte	(809) 721–0865

TRUST TERRITORY OF THE PACIFIC ISLANDS*

Augustine Moses, Acting Chief
OFFICE OF ELDERLY PROGRAMS
Community Development Division
Government of TTPI
Saipan, Mariana Islands 96950
Tel. Nos. 9335 or 9336

AREA AGENCIES

PSA	Area agency address	Director and telephone number
1	Federated States of Micronesia** Area Agency on Aging, National Government, Federated States of Micronesia, Kolonia, Ponape 96941.	Mr. Whens, Billen . . . . 470 (Overseas)
2	Palau Area Agency on Aging, Republic of Palau, Koror, Palau 96940.	Ms. Isabella Sumang . . . . 544 (Overseas)
3	Marshalls Area Agency on Aging, Republic of the Marshall Islands, Majuro, Marshalls 96960.	Mr. Antonio Eliu . . . . 3351 (Overseas)

*Boundaries pending.
**The Federated States of Micronesia consist of: 1. Truk State, 2. Ponape State, 3. Kosrae State, and 4. Yap State.

VIRGIN ISLANDS*

(Federal Region II)

State Agency on Aging

Gloria King, Executive Secretary
COMMISSION ON AGING
6F Havensight Mall - Charlotte Amalie
St. Thomas, Virgin Islands 00801
(809) 774-5884

*The Virgin Islands serves as a single planning and service area.